A Handbook for Teacher Leaders

Leonard O. Pellicer
Lorin W. Anderson

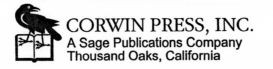
CORWIN PRESS, INC.
A Sage Publications Company
Thousand Oaks, California

For information address:

Corwin Press, Inc.
A Sage Publications Company
2455 Teller Road
Thousand Oaks, California 91320
E-mail: order@corwin.sagepub.com

SAGE Publications, Ltd.
6 Bonhill Street
London EC2AU
United Kingdom

SAGE Publications India Pvt. Ltd.
M-32 Market
Greater Kailash I
New Delhi 110 048 India

Printed in the United States of America

Library of Congress Cataloging-in-Publication Data

Pellicer, Leonard O.
    A handbook for teacher leaders / Leonard D. Pellicer, Lorin W.
    Anderson.
        p. cm.
    Includes bibliographical references and index.
    ISBN 0-8039-6172-3 (cloth: acid-free paper)
    ISBN 0-8039-6173-1 (pbk. acid-free paper)
    1. Teachers—United States—Handbooks, manuals, etc.
2. Educational leadership—United States—Handbooks, manuals, etc.
3. School supervision—United States—Handbooks, manuals, etc.
I. Anderson, Lorin W. II. Title
LB1775.P45 1995
371.1′02—dc20   95-2535

This book is printed on acid-free paper.

00 01 02 03 04 05 10 9 8 7 6 5 4

Corwin Press Production Editor: Diana E. Axelsen
Ventura Typesetter: Janelle LeMaster

Contents

Preface

Purpose of the Book

A handbook for teachers in leadership roles is long overdue. Teacher leaders have been around now for a very long time. In fact, it is a pretty safe bet that no modern school could function effectively without teachers assuming a number of important formal and informal leadership roles. Some of the formal roles, such as department chairpersons and team leaders, have become well established over the years; others, such as lead teachers and master teachers, have rolled in on the crest of the reform waves of the last decade.

As schools have become larger and more complex, principals have simply not been able to maintain total responsibility for the instructional leadership function; many educators would argue that principals were never very effective in this regard. Principals do not have the necessary content expertise, the massive amounts of time required, or the wherewithal to build the trust relationships that are so vital to supervising the performance of teachers across already extremely diverse and ever-expanding fields of knowledge.

Individuals serving in the principalship have always been confounded by the conflicting demands that require them to exercise the dual roles of evaluator and supervisor. Whereas the evaluator role involves making summative judgments to ensure quality control in the instructional program, the supervisor role requires establishing a bond of trust among colleagues and giving and receiving feedback for the purpose of improving instruction. Perhaps it is the conflicting demands of the mutually exclusive roles of evaluator and supervisor that are responsible for the paternalistic attitudes many principals have displayed toward "their" teachers in the past. One thing is quite certain, however: Unless the education community comes to realize the mutual exclusivity of the evaluation and supervision functions, principals will continue the struggle to maintain Jekyll and Hyde personalities in their efforts to satisfy the unreasonable demands placed on them by the system, and instructional leadership will continue to be the empty promise it has always been.

Intended Audience

A Handbook for Teacher Leaders has several intended audiences. The first audience is teachers already in teacher leadership roles. The second includes all teachers who someday will fill such roles. We hope this book will help them understand and acquire the essential knowledge, skills, and abilities required to be effective in discharging the responsibilities associated with instructional leadership. The book is intended to serve also as a general reference for all teachers who have an interest in growing professionally by outlining concepts for working with others to achieve specified educational outcomes; for describing techniques, methods, and materials that have proven to be effective in doing so; and for providing guidance and practice in their use to promote positive change.

Unique Features of the Book

A Handbook for Teacher Leaders is written from the perspective of the teacher leader, rather than from the perspective of the school administrator. The contents were selected carefully on the basis of a thorough review of the current literature in the area of teacher leadership, tempered by our more than 40 years of combined experience in working with teachers, principals, and schools to improve instruction. Topics were included in the book on the basis of how useful teacher leaders have said these would be in helping them work with their fellow teachers to improve instruction.

We tried to make our treatment of the topics both expansive and practical. Our intent was to write in nontechnical, jargon-free language, so far as possible, while providing numerous practical examples to illuminate concepts and ideas. Furthermore, we broke with convention at times when it seemed judicious in meeting our goal to produce a handbook that would talk directly to teacher leaders about instructional leadership. For example, we abandoned the term *instructional supervision* in favor of the expression *instructional leadership*. To us, instructional supervision denotes a hierarchical arrangement in which an all-knowing superior supervises the work of a less knowledgeable subordinate. Such hierarchies have no place in the practice of teacher leadership and are better left to others.

Need for the Book

The discussion of teacher leadership is still rather new. For the past 200 years, American educators have assumed that leadership should be reserved for those occupying formal administrative roles in the educational bureaucracy. Through words and deeds, those who have occupied positions of power have nurtured the pervasive attitude that teachers must devote their energies to the daily tasks of teaching, while leaving the leadership to the principals who have been hired to lead. Because of this exclusivity, the limited leadership opportunities available to teachers in the past were designed primarily to ensure efficiency, rather than to promote leadership.

But a new call for teacher leadership has gone out from a growing throng increasingly dissatisfied with the results of the old ways of doing the business of education. Now, more than ever, it is clear that newer and better ways must be found to "profession-alize teaching" while providing more effective "instructional lead-ership." Some synthesis of these two themes must occur if teachers are to fully realize the potential for either and to thereby substan-tially improve our schools.

Whether or not the principal is perceived as *the instructional leader* in the school is no longer the most relevant concern. A far more pressing issue is whether or not the critical functions related to instructional leadership are being performed effectively by some person or persons in the school. Teachers are unquestionably the best and most abundant source of instructional leadership available to schools. It is our sincerest wish that *A Handbook for Teacher Leaders* will prove helpful to those teachers who must assume a larger measure of responsibility for improving educa-tional programs, instructional techniques, and other related ser-vices for children.

Scope and Treatment

This book is divided into three parts, each consisting of three chapters. Part One, "The Nature of School Leadership," is devoted to a description of teacher leaders and how they lead. Chapter 1 describes the results of the major research studies of teacher lead-ers, outlines some of the more persistent obstacles to achieving effective teacher leadership, and defines the nature of instruc-tional leadership. Chapter 2 describes how teacher leaders can successfully go about establishing a "helping relationship" with their colleagues. Chapter 3 explores the philosophical basis for instructional programs in schools and suggests ways for teacher leaders to help bring about substantive improvement while effec-tively evaluating the results of their efforts.

Part Two, "The Instructional Process," is devoted to providing the information that teacher leaders need to help them work with their colleagues in improving instruction in individual class-rooms. Chapters are included on planning, presenting, and evalu-ating instruction.

Part Three, "Teachers Working Together to Reclaim Schools," is dedicated to helping teachers grow professionally, with the ultimate aim of assisting them in reclaiming their birthright as the true and rightful leaders of schools. Chapter 7 provides information to help teacher leaders understand and implement effective staff development programs with their fellow teachers. Chapter 8 describes peer coaching, complete with instructions on how to get a program started in a school. Chapter 9, the concluding chapter, covers reform, restructuring, and renewal. It focuses on confronting and overcoming the barriers to teacher leadership suggested in the initial chapter. This final chapter is intended to help teachers create a vision for the kind of schools we need and to accept responsibility and accountability for seeing that the changes necessary to achieve the vision actually come about.

Acknowledgments

We wish to thank all who contributed to the completion of this labor of love. To our editor, Alice Foster, we want you to know that you are very good at your job. Although on numerous occasions we disagreed, you never wavered in your determination to help us produce a finished product that both recognized and respected the importance of teacher leadership to the future of American education. Although we hate to admit it, Alice, you were right the great majority of the time! Thank you for your dedication, commitment, and professionalism.

We want to express our deepest respect and admiration to our friend and colleague Aretha Pigford for her help in conceptualizing this project, as well as for her significant contributions to Chapter 5. We also want to acknowledge the special assistance we received from Kathleen Milligan and Diane Harwell in researching material for the book, as well as in reading and editing our work, and to Susan Fortune and Cathy Schachner for their help in the layout and design of certain sections of the book, as well as in the typing and correction of manuscripts. A special thank you is extended to Istafanus Sanga for the help he provided in indexing.

Finally, we want to express our deepest heartfelt appreciation to all of the teacher leaders who contributed their thoughts and ideas to this project. Most are toiling away in their classrooms with their students every day. Others are in special leadership roles that have temporarily pulled them away from daily contact with their students. Still others have taken up the gauntlet and are championing the cause of teacher leadership through teaching and writing and speaking about it in every corner of this great land. Regardless of their roles, all are making important contributions to the future well-being of education in our nation. We thank you.

Leonard O. Pellicer
Lorin W. Anderson

About the Authors

Leonard O. Pellicer is Chair of the Department of Educational Leadership and Policies and Professor of Educational Administration at the University of South Carolina, where he has been a faculty member since 1978. His experience includes teaching in middle and high schools, serving as an assistant principal and a principal at the high school level, and serving as director of a Teacher Education Center serving teachers and administrators in five Florida school districts. He served as director of the South Carolina Educational Policy Center from 1987-1994, and consulted and taught during the past 3 years in the Republic of South Africa in the area of school leadership. He received a B.A. in English education (1969) and master's (1971) and doctoral (1973) degrees in educational administration at the University of Florida. He was selected and served as a Fulbright Scholar to the Southeast Asian region during 1986-1987, where his expertise was instrumental in developing school leaders in the region. He has written, consulted, and spoken extensively in the areas of instructional leadership, school leadership, and educational programs for disadvantaged students. He chaired a 10-year study for the National Association of Secondary School Principals that resulted in two widely read volumes: *High School Leaders and Their Schools: The National Profile*

(1988) and *High School Leaders and Their Schools: Profiles of Effectiveness* (1990).

Lorin W. Anderson is a Carolina Research Professor in the Department of Educational Leadership and Policies at the University of South Carolina. He teaches graduate courses in general curriculum, research design, and college teaching, and has written and consulted extensively in the areas of classroom instruction, school learning, and educational programs for children who are economically disadvantaged. He received a B.A. in mathematics from Macalester College in 1963 and began his career in education as a secondary mathematics teacher in a small town in northern Minnesota. After 2 years, he moved to a suburb of Minneapolis, where he taught junior high mathematics for 2 years. He completed his master's degree at the University of Minnesota in 1971 and left public school teaching to attend the University of Chicago, where he studied with Benjamin S. Bloom. On receipt of his doctoral degree in 1973, he moved to South Carolina, where he has served on the faculty of the College of Education for the past 20 years. His most recent book is *Bloom's Taxonomy: A Forty-Year Retrospective* (1994). He also has edited the monograph *Time Piece: Extending and Enhancing Learning Time* (1993) and has written the monograph *Increasing Teacher Effectiveness* (1992).

PART ONE

The Nature of School Leadership

1

Who Will Be
Leading Our Schools?

*Teaching is not a profession that values or encourages
leadership within its ranks. The hierarchical nature of
public schools is based on the 19th century industrial
model, with the consequent adversarial relationship of
administration as management and teachers as labor.*

(Troen & Boles, 1994, p. 40)

Missed Opportunities

The rigid, bureaucratic, organizational structure encouraged by
the kind of thinking described above has been largely responsible,
during the last century, for preventing teachers from exercising the
kind of leadership that could bring about the long-awaited rebirth
of schooling in America. Although teachers traditionally have had
limited authority to exercise control over conditions that affect
students in their classrooms, school boards and administrators
traditionally have exercised almost total control over conditions
that have affected the working lives of teachers. The results should
have been all too predictable: stagnation of the teaching profession
and the failure of American schools.

Describing the professional lives of teachers through the eyes of the teachers they interviewed, McLaughlin and her colleagues place the blame for the failure of American schools on an educational system that is "structured to guarantee the failure of teachers" (McLaughlin, Pfeifer, Swanson-Owens, & Yee, 1986, p. 420). Teachers must cope with classes that are too large, students who have varying ability levels and widely divergent needs, shortages of teaching resources, isolation from their colleagues, lack of recognition, and unrealistic demands from society and superiors.

These circumstances have led teachers to experience overwhelming feelings of anger, depression, and frustration. If one were to ask these teachers, "Who's leading our schools?" their responses might well be included under one of several equally depressing rubrics: "I really don't know" or "No one is leading our schools"; or perhaps they would respond with the question "Who cares?"

Sykes (1987) noted that teachers face some of the same constraints as other public servants. These include the chronic shortage of supplies and resources, the pursuit of ambiguous and hard-to-evaluate goals, and the charge to deliver personal services in a large, impersonal bureaucracy. But the teaching profession is saddled with additional constraints. Teachers traditionally have been socialized to focus on psychic rewards, rather than on extrinsic ones. They are expected to work in uncertain situations with relatively low salaries and few career opportunities. Perhaps most difficult of all, they work in isolation from other adults and with conscripted clients.

Shedd and Bacharach (1991), while noting that the lack of time and money are serious problems in the professional lives of teachers, pointed out that the "real culprits are the work calendars, time schedules, staffing practices, and physical structures that prevent teachers from working with each other more closely" (p. 94). Wasley (1991) noted that teachers have long worked in a highly regulated system that has minimized the importance of professional judgment while causing teachers simply to follow directions.

Little (1988) described school teaching as characteristically "professional work; it is complex and subtle, requiring informed judgment by well-prepared practitioners in circumstances that are often ambiguous or difficult" (p. 81). But, unfortunately, the current structure of schooling has not supported professionalizing teaching because it "restricts opportunities for joint study and problem solving when complex issues are tackled primarily through the exercise of bureaucratic rule making" (pp. 81-82).

Given the conditions described above, how can anyone reasonably expect that teachers will embrace emerging opportunities to provide much-needed leadership in the schools? If something is not done soon to professionalize teaching, American schools may well be faced with the most serious teacher shortage ever witnessed (Darling-Hammond, 1984). Many of the best teachers are leaving the profession after only a few years in the classroom, and fewer talented young people are entering (Sykes, 1983). Increasingly, difficult-to-educate students, undesirable working conditions, limited extrinsic and intrinsic rewards, and a broader selection of attractive career options for minorities and women have combined to make it imperative for educators to rethink the nature and purpose of schools and teaching. This rumination will require a new kind of leadership—by teachers, for teachers.

Teachers Have Always Been Leaders

The false assumption that teaching is for teachers and that leading is for principals has worked to the disadvantage of American education for a very long time. However, in the period before schools grew large enough to warrant the designation of selected teachers as headmasters or headmistresses, and later, principals, full-time classroom teachers did all of the teaching, as well as most of the leading. They also stoked the fire in the pot-bellied stove, swept the floors, and carried the water.

But over the years, increases and concentrations in school-age populations caused schools to experience dramatic growth. With that growth came equally dramatic structural changes. Although teaching and leading once were considered to be synonymous, they began to be perceived as a dichotomy. Principals and headmasters were employed to see to the running of the schools, and teachers slowly but surely were relegated to carrying out their instructional duties isolated within their classrooms.

Even though the majority of educators may not regard leading and teaching as synonymous, most would freely admit that teaching inherently involves leading (Lynch & Strodl, 1991). At the classroom level, teaching requires setting goals, establishing objectives, selecting and implementing strategies and techniques for achieving those objectives, and evaluating the entire process in terms of its effectiveness. Teachers, while employing limited resources, must also find ways to motivate and inspire reluctant learners to persevere and to put forth the effort required to successfully reach the objectives.

Berliner (1983) likened teachers to executives and suggested that they must perform nine executive functions to be successful in their schools and classrooms: planning, communicating goals, regulating the activities of the workplace, creating a pleasant environment for work, educating new members of the work group, relating the work of the site to other units in the system, supervising and working with other people, motivating those being supervised, and evaluating the performance of those being supervised. From his analysis of teaching, Berliner concluded, "Classrooms are workplaces; complex and dynamic workplaces that require management by an executive of considerable talent. Teachers are not usually thought of as executives. But it's time they became recognized as such" (p. 28).

In addition to the obvious leadership behaviors they display in their classrooms, teachers have for more than a century assumed formal leadership roles in the schools. Department chairpersons, team leaders, grade-level chairpersons, lead teachers, curriculum coordinators, consultants, master teachers, and mentors are just a few of the important formal leadership roles fulfilled by teachers over the years. Hatfield, Blackman, Claypool, and Master (1987) estimated that from 10% to 20% of the teaching staff are engaged in leadership roles designated by more than 50 titles. In these formal roles, as well as in a variety of less formal roles such as members or chairpersons of informal study groups and committees, teachers have served as planners, initiators, developers, facilitators, promoters, ombudsmen, problem solvers, nurturers, values clarifiers, and catalysts for individual as well as school-wide improvement. Without question, teachers have always been leaders regardless of whether or not their leadership has been fully acknowledged.

The Reform and Restructuring of Schools

Recent years have witnessed a mountain of reports from an assortment of commissions, task forces, and committees, declaring that American education is broken and suggesting alternatives for fixing it. *A Nation at Risk: The Imperative for Education Reform*, produced by the National Commission on Excellence in Education (1983), was the first such report to gain wide attention and sparked a flood of similar reports. Among the most frequently mentioned recommendations for substantial school improvement contained in these reports is the replacement of the outmoded bureaucratic educational structure that precludes taking full advantage of the tremendous potential that exists for teacher leadership. In its 1986 report *A Nation Prepared: Teachers for the 21st Century*, the Carnegie Foundation for the Advancement of Teaching declared, "The key [to successful reform of schools] lies in creating a new profession . . . of well-educated teachers prepared to assume new powers and responsibilities to redesign schools for the future" (p. 2).

This call for restructuring schools "raises issues of fundamental change in the way teachers are prepared, inducted into teaching, and involved in leadership and decision making at the school level" (Lieberman, 1988, p. 4). Restructuring represents an important evolution in thinking about education because the underlying assumption is that the problem of American education resides in the structure of schools and in the roles of teachers in schools, not in the curriculum, academic standards, or accountability measures.

Although a number of forces have been driving the educational establishment toward a reconceptualization of schools and schooling, the extent to which it is possible to effectively restructure American public school education may well depend primarily on educators' ability to change their conceptualization of teachers and the conditions in which they work. As it is currently structured and practiced, many thoughtful observers would not even consider teaching to be a true profession.

> Definitions of "professional" practice commonly agree that professionals develop a specialized knowledge base from which appropriate decisions can be made on behalf of clients; that professionals have the ability to apply that knowledge in individual, nonroutine circumstances; and that they have a strong ethical commitment to do what is best for the client. In addition, according to common definitions, professionals usually work together to determine the requirements of credentialing and licensure. Current research illustrates that it is difficult to describe teaching using these definitions. (Wasley, 1991, p. 16)

Schools and the Factory Metaphor

In the not-too-distant past, the mission of American schools was relatively simple. For the most part, schools existed to expose children to and help them master a narrowly defined curriculum, one dominated by the three Rs and essentially designed to provide students with the basic knowledge and skills they needed to function in an agrarian, and later, industrial, society. This single curriculum was intended for a single group of students. No special education programs, gifted programs, or compensatory programs were available. Because the curriculum was not designed to accommodate different student aptitudes, interests, or needs, many students simply dropped out of school at an early age to pursue a livelihood.

During these "good old days" of American public school education, few support services were available to students. Times were simple, and school support services reflected this simplicity. Two-parent families were the norm. Big-city blight, drug abuse, and gang warfare, though not unheard of, were certainly not the massive social problems they have become today. There were no "crack babies," and although they may have existed, children with fetal alcohol syndrome were unknown to educators. Parents were expected to take personal responsibility to see that their children got to and from school, had the food they needed to sustain them throughout the day, and received the discipline and counseling they required to solve their educational, social, and career problems.

Within this relatively simple world, schools operated like a factory (Livingston, 1992). Education was an extremely bureaucratic, highly rationalized enterprise dominated by the thinking and philosophy that grew out of the scientific management era. Standardized outcomes were defined in terms of efficiency and effectiveness. Tight supervision was the norm, with principals closely supervising teachers to ensure compliance with what was believed to be "best practice." Principals were the acknowledged leaders of schools and were given authority for making decisions; teachers were expected to carry out unquestioningly those decisions while teaching their students who, in turn, were the products of the same hierarchical educational system and process.

The industrial model has hampered the development of American education for a very long time. To think that this factory metaphor has been highly descriptive of the heart of the American system of public education until the dawn of the 21st century is nothing short of incredible! It "does not account adequately for the complexity of schools as they exist, and certainly not for what we wish them to be" (Livingston, 1992, p. 12).

Perhaps one of the major reasons the legislated reforms of the 1980s had such slight impact on the practice and performance of American education is that these reforms were very much in keeping with the factory metaphor. Rather than reform the workplace, the wave of reform legislation simply mandated that educators do what they had always done—but do more of it better.

Because recent reform efforts have been couched within the factory metaphor, some very negative, unintended side effects have resulted. For example, more academic courses were added to the requirements for graduation, more days were added to the school calendar, and more tests (including exit examinations) were devised to measure students' progress. Coincidentally, more work and stress were added to the already difficult job of teaching, while at the same time requirements to enter the teaching profession were systematically raised. Buckling to the demands of the business community, the education community tested numerous schemes to "encourage" teachers to work harder and to be more professional through the creation of career ladders and teacher incentive and merit pay systems. But the basic bureaucratic structure of education did not change noticeably. School principals still were regarded as the leaders, and teachers still were regarded as the line workers. Rather than revitalize teaching as was intended, these pseudo-reforms further drained the vitality from the teaching profession by making teaching even more difficult than it was before, while ensuring the continued isolation of teachers from one another, thereby forcing them to do their difficult work alone. Furthermore, the legion of ill-advised and poorly implemented teacher incentive and merit pay systems created an antagonistic "we-they" relationship among teachers and between teachers and administrators.

Teacher Autonomy and Its Consequences

The highly bureaucratic, top-down structure of schools has resulted in a level of teacher autonomy that has led to teacher isolation, alienation, and disenchantment. As Bidwell (1965) suggested, "Teacher autonomy is reflected in the structure of school systems, resulting in what might be called their structural looseness. The teacher works alone within the classroom, relatively hidden from colleagues and superiors, so that he has a broad discretional jurisdiction within the boundaries of the classroom" (p. 976).

A decade later, Weick (1976) coined the phrase "loosely coupled" to describe the structural looseness mentioned by Bidwell. Lortie (1975) and Meyer and Rowan (1978) documented the loosely coupled nature of schools and school systems.

This structure of schools affects the relationships among teachers, as well as the relationships between teachers and administrators. It is unusual for teachers to have opportunities to talk with one another about students, schools, or teaching. In many schools, a general lack of agreement is evident between teachers and administrators as to primary goals, policies, and procedures (Deal & Celotti, 1977). The sad reality is that teachers and principals simply do not discuss such matters on a regular basis. Policies, even when written, tend to be implemented inconsistently. Minimum interpersonal contact, lack of agreement on goals and procedures, and inconsistencies in their understanding and implementation are all indications of a loosely coupled organization. Thus, although teachers have the luxury of working alone, it is precisely because they work alone that no one seems to know or appreciate exactly what they do or accomplish.

One negative consequence of teacher autonomy and isolation is a feeling of disenchantment and alienation experienced by many teachers. As has been mentioned, teachers gain their autonomy by virtue of being members of loosely coupled organizations. This loose coupling refers not only to the absence of formal linkages between individuals at different levels of the organization but also to a lack of agreement among organizational members as to their roles and responsibilities, as well as how to implement policies and procedures.

With a lack of agreement about roles, responsibilities, policies, and procedures, conflicts between teachers and administrators and among teachers themselves are likely to occur. Everyone in the organization is likely to be operating under a different set of assumptions, precepts, and images. These differences can and often do breed distrust and cause people dedicated to the same course to step unknowingly on each other's toes (Deal & Celotti, 1977).

In loosely coupled organizations, the channels of authority are often unclear and confused. The question of who's in charge is frequently raised. The most frequent answer is either, "I don't know" or "Nobody!" In situations like this, the design and implementation of meaningful and productive school leadership roles for teachers may be far more difficult than they were in the past.

As Wasley (1991) pointed out, "Traditional leadership opportunities for teachers are extremely limited and generally serve an efficiency function rather than a leadership function" (p. 4).

This combination of loosely coupled organizations, distrust, and a perceived lack of someone "in charge" is likely to result in feelings of alienation—that is, a feeling that a person is "powerless to achieve the role that he [or she] has determined to be rightfully his [or hers] in specific situations" (Cox & Wood, 1980, p. 1). Thus the very autonomy that permits teachers to "do their own thing" in their classrooms causes numerous problems in the world outside their classrooms.

In combination, loosely coupled organizations and teacher autonomy provide a breeding ground for maintaining the status quo. It should not be surprising, then, that meaningful, sustained improvements in instructional practices have been rare. The combination of loosely coupled organizations and teacher autonomy contributes to the frequent turnover of educational innovations. As Deal and Celotti (1977) noted, "Without an ongoing supportive structure, teachers are free to experiment according to personal commitment—or whim—and then to let the initial momentum dwindle, soon to be replaced by another inspiration" (p. 20).

Professionalizing Teaching

We have discussed the factory model of schooling and the impact it has had on deprofessionalizing teaching. It is clear that teaching can never be regarded as a true profession as long as people cling to the notion that principals are the managers of the school enterprise and that teachers are the workers. This view presents an insurmountable obstacle to tapping the vast leadership resources available in the teaching force and cripples any attempts to truly restructure schools.

During the educational reform in the 1980s, a great deal of attention was focused on the role of the principal as the instructional leader of the school. Goals were set for schools, and the principal was entrusted with the responsibility to drive the organization toward the realization of these goals. More recently, however, the realization has been growing that this reformist approach has not worked. It has become increasingly clear that principals cannot supply all of the leadership needed to reform schools.

The focus now has shifted from reform to restructured schools. The notion of restructuring calls for shared leadership and responsibility by principals and teachers. Under this approach, the principal's most important task must be to organize and cultivate the talents of all of the players in the school, thus providing a dynamic new kind of leadership. In restructured schools, teachers' roles must be expanded; teachers must make decisions that affect not only the students in their classrooms but also the working lives of everyone else in the school.

The reaction to this new role for teachers has been mixed. Although some teachers have willingly embraced it, others have been more hesitant. Even those who have embraced it have serious questions about how their new roles and responsibilities should be defined. Many lack confidence in their ability to perform some of the new tasks expected of them. Although many teachers have consistently demonstrated their ability to lead, some have not had an ample opportunity to develop and practice leadership skills. Some prospective teacher leaders fear the chasm the new roles might place between them and their colleagues; others are called on to assume responsibility but are unsure of the authority they have been given or whether they even want authority. In many settings, teacher leadership roles are still ambiguous, and many teachers are frightened by that ambiguity.

If teachers are to get past these fears and to function as true professionals, then principals must change the way they themselves function. Both principals and teachers must abandon the false assumption that the principal is the instructional leader in the school and realize that everyone must take responsibility for providing such leadership. Principals must make it a priority to secure, maintain, and provide an adequate array of resources and support services that will enable teachers to perform the work for which they have been certified and employed. The expectation is also that an articulation of ethical norms will be practiced throughout the organization to help guide the professionals in the conduct of their work.

Rather than rely exclusively on principals to evaluate teacher job performance, school boards and superintendents would do well to adopt the view that teachers are professionals who are willing and able to share power and authority through implementing a system of peer review much like the ones used at colleges and universities. This process effectively transfers the responsibility for professional conduct to the professionals, which ultimately prevents malpractice and encourages public respect.

If the education community truly desires to professionalize teaching, then it must alter its conception of teachers and teaching. In this regard, some of the fundamental practices and policies that presently encourage the rationalization or routinization of teaching must be changed. School leaders must dispense with ineffective evaluation systems that fail to recognize the complexity of teaching, spurn peer review, and cause principals to act as supervisors. They must halt competition for teacher loyalty and eliminate teacher isolation by bringing professional educators together to engage in meaningful dialogue. They must regard the work of teaching as mission-bound, rather than as time-bound.

Most important, however, school leaders must shift a major portion of the responsibility for leadership from principals to teachers. Such a shift enables principals to do better what they do (be administrators), while at the same time permits teachers to do better what they do best (make and act on decisions in the best interest of their students). Lieberman, Saxl, and Miles (1988) cut to the heart of the matter:

> It is paradoxical that, although teachers spend most of their time facilitating for student learning, they themselves have few people facilitating for them and understanding their needs to be recognized, encouraged, helped, supported, and engaged in professional learning. Perhaps this is what we mean by "professionalizing" teaching and "restructuring the work environment" of teachers. (p. 152)

As Little (1988) noted, even the most conservative workplace reform proposals require teachers to "act differently toward their work and one another . . ." and "to take the *lead* [italics added] in advancing the understanding and practice of teaching" (p. 82).

What Is Instructional Leadership, and Who Really Provides It?

A few years ago, we were part of a national research team that conducted an in-depth study of instructional leadership in American high schools (Pellicer, Anderson, Keefe, Kelley, & McCleary, 1990). Initially, our expectations were that, in accordance with the general thinking and attitudes reflected in the profession at that time, principals would assume primary responsibility for instructional leadership and be recognized as instructional leaders in their schools. But that turned out not to be the case. We discovered convincing evidence that instructional leadership, at least in the most effective schools, was a shared responsibility. In no instance was the principal the sole source of instructional leadership, and only in isolated instances could the principal be characterized as a primary source. Surprisingly, most teachers told us that they "never sought the advice of the principal in instructional matters" and that discussions of instructional improvements tended to be "department centered," rather than "school centered." More often than not, department chairpersons were identified as the major source of instructional leadership in the secondary schools we studied.

So what is instructional leadership? What is it that principals were not doing and that teachers were? These are difficult questions to answer even for those actively engaged in the process (Pellicer et al., 1990). In many ways, it is easier to define what instructional leadership is *not*.

Instructional leadership is not a set of discrete behaviors or activities, such as ordering curricular materials, monitoring and evaluating teaching, and designing staff development activities. Educators who believe that instructional leadership is simply doing things related to instruction devote all of their time to *doing instructional things*. And although all of these activities can be directly related to instructional leadership, in isolation they are not instructional leadership. Instructional leadership is not just doing things, even important and worthwhile things, related to instruction.

Nor is instructional leadership just an attitude. Many people think instructional leadership is an attitude that can be exercised by verbal expression. Those who think instructional leadership is an attitude say things like, "Instruction is the most important thing in the school," or "Everything we do in this school must somehow relate to and improve the instructional program." They act as if instructional leadership is verbally contagious and that by expressing such sentiments repeatedly, they will cause others in the school to be infected with the spirit and the desire to work hard and improve the instructional program. But words become meaningless without action to back them up. Instructional leadership is more than simply *saying instructional things.*

If instructional leadership is not a set of discrete activities and behaviors or simply an expressed attitude, then what is it?

More than 40 years of combined experience and research have led us to define *instructional leadership* as the *initiation and implementation of planned change in a school's instructional program, supported by the various constituencies in the school, that results in substantial and sustained improvement in student learning.*

The exercise of instructional leadership calls for providing vision and direction, resources and support to both teachers and students. As we wrote a few years ago, "Instructional leadership begins with an attitude, an expressed commitment to student growth and productivity, from which emanates values, behaviors, and functions deliberately designed to foster, facilitate, and support student satisfaction and achievement" (Pellicer et al., 1990, p. 31).

Although we are quite sure that effective schools require instructional leadership, we are equally sure that instructional leadership does not necessarily begin and end with the principal. Rather, instructional leadership must come from teachers if schools are to improve and if teaching is to achieve professional status. This assertion raises one final question: What do we know about teacher leaders that can provide us with the basis for improving teacher leadership?

Teachers Who Lead

As already noted, teachers who lead occupy positions with a variety of titles. We believe the title is relatively unimportant. Whether a teacher leader is titled lead teacher, department chairman, grade chairwoman, curriculum coordinating teacher, master teacher, or whatever is less important than the functions the leader performs and the ability of the leader to establish and maintain acceptance and credibility with those he or she leads. Leadership involves change, and change requires the ability to take others where they would not normally go. Wasley (1991) defined teacher leadership as "the ability . . . to engage colleagues in experimentation and then examination of more powerful instructional practices in the service of more engaged student learning" (p. 170). We like this definition; it is focused on children and instruction and denotes change in a positive direction.

To function as leaders, teachers who lead engage in a wide variety of behaviors. They assume responsibility for the continued development of their professional colleagues. They mentor those new to the profession by serving as role models. They provide leadership in content areas by producing instructional materials and creating positive work environments under trying circumstances. And teacher leaders engage in these leadership activities while continuing to teach their own classes of students (Lieberman, 1988; Wasley, 1991).

Lieberman et al. (1988) added to and expanded on this list of teacher leadership roles and responsibilities. In a multiyear study of 17 teachers in a variety of teacher leadership roles, they found that successful teacher leaders employed a set of skill clusters that allowed them to (a) build trust and rapport, (b) examine issues within an organization context, (c) build skill and confidence in others, (d) use resources wisely and efficiently, (e) deal with the change process, and (f) engage in collaborative work with teaching colleagues. From the results of their study, they concluded that "finding ways to create structures for teachers to work together, to focus on the problems of their school, to enhance their repertoires of teaching strategies—all are part of the work of teachers who work with other teachers" (Lieberman, 1988, p. 6).

O'Connor and Boles (1992) reported the results of a survey of Massachusetts teacher leaders on the nature of their roles and the support they needed to be successful in those roles. The researchers found that a significant majority of their sample of teacher leaders was involved in curriculum leadership, grade-level or department decision making, and staff development. The vast majority had conducted workshops and seminars for other teachers, and most had served as mentors for other teachers. The major roadblocks to effectiveness in their leadership roles were a lack of time, unsatisfactory relationships with other teachers and administrators, and a lack of money to get the job done. In terms of the additional skills and knowledge they needed in order to be more effective, teacher leaders in Massachusetts cited the need for a better understanding of the politics of schools, power, authority, interpersonal relationships, communications skills, group dynamics, presentation skills, organizational skills, and change.

Wasley (1991), in her revealing in-depth study of three teacher leaders, was struck "by how enormously complex teacher leadership roles are as they play out in practice" (p. 154). She noted that the roles involved power, authority, decision making, and different kinds of collaboration. Wasley's work strongly reinforces the notion that both teaching and leading are exhausting—even more so when they are done simultaneously. Furthermore, in most cases, there are no real incentives for teachers to lead; they lead because they believe in what they are trying to accomplish.

Established teacher leadership roles, such as department chairpersons and team leaders, when contrasted with emerging teacher leadership roles, such as those highlighted in Wasley's study of teacher leaders, can lead to significant role confusion. Teacher leaders are teachers first, but they also are rare individuals who differ in significant ways from many of their colleagues. It is not surprising that all of these circumstances together can mean that the intentions for teacher leadership roles may not match the realities. Paradoxically, the confusion surrounding emerging teacher leadership roles led Wasley to conclude that the "factors that enabled the teacher leaders to be successful with their colleagues also constrained them, at once enhancing and diminishing their potential" (p. 154).

Hatfield et al. (1987), in a study of the characteristics, activities, responsibilities, and organizational conditions affecting teacher leaders, identified the following skills and qualities as important to their work: (a) the ability to deal with people, (b) the ability to communicate well, (c) flexibility and patience, (d) technical competence, and (e) the ability to be respected. The study revealed that the major responsibilities of teacher leaders centered on staff development, curricular development, and instructional improvement.

The Challenge Ahead

Creating the revolutionary organizational structures needed to promote the kind of teacher leadership envisioned by those at the forefront of educational restructuring will not be a simple task. Old ways die hard. Redefining roles in ways that encourage teachers to assume major responsibilities for instructional leadership is a tall order for many in the educational establishment. Moving away from the factory model of schooling requires no less than a major paradigm shift, a revolution in thinking that many teachers, principals, superintendents, board members, and especially legislators may not yet be prepared to embrace.

But if teacher leadership is to play a significant role in the genuine renewal of schools and schooling in this country, then education professionals must expect the challenge to be difficult. They must recognize that significant social change rarely occurs suddenly. How long has American society been struggling to desegregate society? To ensure equality for women? To combat alcohol and drug abuse? Complex structural changes on the scale and of the significance required to substantially alter the way schools do business will be no less challenging than issues relating to desegregation, equality, or substance abuse. Everyone must realize that real change—the kind of change discussed here—must occur in the hearts and minds of individuals, not in the policies of institutions. When enough individual hearts and minds change, then policies will change with them.

Even if educators are successful in reconceptualizing the way schools should be organized, they still must address a number of important issues before they can realize the goal of creating significant leadership roles for teachers on a large scale. The "egalitarian ethic" that encourages educators to think of every teacher as being just like every other teacher regardless of "how experienced, how effective, or how knowledgeable" individual teachers may be remains a major obstacle to designing meaningful teacher leadership roles (Lieberman, 1988, p. 7). The isolation imposed on teachers by the way work responsibilities are divided, time schedules and work calendars are arranged, and buildings are designed continues to prevent them from active participation in the discussion of educational reform. And turf wars between bureaucratic school hierarchies and powerful teacher organizations initially spawned to protect teacher rights and privileges now stand in the way of real collaborative relationships that embrace the entire educational community.

Although these issues will not be resolved easily, the potential rewards are more than worth the effort. The end of forced teacher isolation and the building of colleagueship among teachers and between teachers and principals can be achieved. Greater recognition and enhancement of the status for teachers, a more favorable system of teacher rewards, and the building of more flexible and responsive school structures to reshape teaching as an occupation can improve the work lives of teachers and encourage greater numbers of talented young people to pursue teaching as a career (Lieberman, 1988, p. 8). Perhaps most important, a realization of the potential for teacher leadership can truly professionalize teaching and revolutionize schooling in America. On the basis of our reading and our own work with hundreds of teacher leaders over the years, we have arrived at two major conclusions. First, if schools are to be restructured successfully, teachers must assume a variety of important instructional leadership responsibilities. Second, many teachers are willing to assume these responsibilities but have not been adequately prepared in terms of the knowledge, skills, and attitudes required to function as instructional leaders within loosely coupled school organizations.

The purpose of this volume is to provide current and prospective teacher leaders with the knowledge, skills, and attitudes they need in order to carry out their instructional leadership roles effectively. The remaining chapters provide a balance of content (what teacher leaders need to know) and process (ways they can use this knowledge most effectively).

Without question, teachers are the best and most abundant source of leadership available to schools. Teacher leaders remain the last best hope for significantly improving American education. If teachers fail to embrace their responsibility to provide the leadership needed in our schools, then all educators fail. And if administrative bureaucrats do not provide the conditions and support necessary for teacher leadership to flourish, then all educators fail. In the final analysis, the efforts of teacher leaders at the forefront of change will be only as successful as the bureaucracy *allows* them to be!

> Our experience has proven to us that it is absolutely vital that teachers remake the profession and establish a culture in which classroom teachers are seen as fully empowered partners in shaping policy, creating curriculum, managing budgets, improving practice, and bringing added value toward the goal of improving education for children. (Troen & Boles, 1994, p. 40)

2

Creating a
Helping Relationship

Being dependent on others is an integral part of the human condition. No one is so self-reliant that he or she never needs to depend on another person for help or assistance in a variety of serious and not-so-serious situations. But what exactly is help? What gives some human beings the power to help other human beings? Why and how do they choose to exercise this power to help others? And what determines whether or not proffered help will be accepted and how the recipient feels about the help received? Although these questions may be simple, the answers are rather complex. The answers are also very important to those whose goal it is to be effective teacher leaders.

Leadership—any kind of leadership—is concerned with helping. Teacher leadership is concerned with teachers helping teachers so that teachers can, in turn, better help students. Teacher leadership is helping teachers work together to establish and achieve the goals and objectives of the school. If teacher leaders are to be successful in helping teachers in this way, they must have a basic understanding of what it means to provide help in the context of the complexity of human relationships. This chapter is a discussion of the nature of help and what it truly means to be helpful.

Suppose, for a moment, that you are driving home from an out-of-town meeting late one night along an unfamiliar road. Torrential rain is obstructing your vision. Before you know it, you have taken a wrong turn and you find yourself on a deserted country road. Suddenly, you hear a muffled explosion, and your car starts bumping and becomes difficult to steer. Oh no! Talk about bad timing! You have a blowout on the right front tire. To make matters worse, you don't know how to change a tire. No question about it; you need help!

You sit in your car for an hour and a half, worrying about how you are going to get out of this mess. Your family will be frantic when you don't arrive home all night. They will be calling every hospital in the state and will have the highway patrol out searching for you in all the ditches. You've never felt so helpless. You curse yourself for your inability to change a tire and vow to correct this little shortcoming just as soon as you are safe and sound—if you are ever safe and sound again! Finally, you see two headlights approaching. As the headlights draw nearer, you see that it's an old pickup truck. The truck lurches to a stop; a big, burly man in overalls gets out and lumbers over to the driver's side of your car. You roll down the car window just a tiny bit, and the man asks if you're having trouble. You tell him about your flat and admit that you don't know how to change a tire. He tugs on his unkempt beard for a moment or two and then tells you he can change a tire; that is, he "can change a tyre for a hunnert dollars!" You're in a desperate situation, so you reluctantly agree to meet the stranger's demand and he fixes your flat tire.

Now suppose that you are in the same situation—same rainy night, same flat tire, same feeling of distress, same old pickup truck, same burly man. Only one thing is different: When you roll down your car window just a tiny bit and admit your helplessness, the man doesn't mention money. He tells you he can change the tire, rolls up the sleeves on his dungaree work shirt, and proceeds to do so. After the tire is finally changed, the man is standing there soaking wet. You roll down your window a little farther and thank him from the bottom of your heart. In fact, you do more than thank him. You take out your checkbook and proceed to write him a check for $100. The stranger protests vigorously even though you can see that he probably needs the money. Finally, you convince him that his help was worth ten times as much as you're paying him, and he reluctantly accepts the check.

Let's analyze how you might have felt and why you might have felt that way in the two situations described above. Although the circumstances were essentially identical and the end result was the same, chances are that your feelings would have been quite different in the two situations. In the first instance, when the stranger demanded money to "help" you, most likely you would have felt a strong sense of resentment because you were vulnerable and another person exploited that vulnerability. If you were relating the incident about the flat tire to a friend at a later date, it is highly doubtful that you would have used the word *help* to describe what took place that night; you didn't feel helped. You felt exploited.

In the second instance, your feelings likely would have been much different. Although the stranger surely recognized your vulnerability, he chose not to exploit it; rather, he acted in a way that allowed you to maintain your dignity. Because of the way he acted, you felt that you were in control of the situation, and in the end, you were even in a position to reciprocate for the help that was extended to you by voluntarily paying the stranger for his time and assistance. The tangible results were the same as in the first instance: You paid $100 to have your flat tire fixed. But the intangible results, the feelings you experienced, were probably much different. Relating the event to a friend later, you might have described a kind and thoughtful stranger who went out of his way to help you out of a tight spot.

Motivation: A Key to Helping

Why do human beings help each other? What determines whether or not proffered help will be accepted and how the recipient will feel about the help he or she receives? We think the answers to these questions involve the motives of the helper and how the recipient of the help interprets those motives.

Human beings help one another for a variety of reasons— some noble, some not so noble. Most people recognize altruism as a prime motivation for many caring and helpful acts. In many situations, people help simply because they see someone in need and think it is the right thing to do. Perhaps religious training or exposure to parental, cultural, or community values have helped shape the inclination of most people to provide help to those they see in need. When altruism is the motive for helping, the helper does not really want or expect to receive anything in return. The feeling that he or she has done the right thing through helping another human being is reward enough for helping. Helping an elderly person across the street, giving freely to a charitable organization, and providing canned goods for the food bank can all be examples of helping because of altruistic motivations.

But, there are many other motives for helping besides altruism. Sometimes people help because it is their job to help. Firefighters do not go into burning buildings and rescue people primarily for altruistic reasons; they go into burning buildings and rescue people because they are trained and paid to do exactly that. This is not to say that no altruism is involved in fire fighting (especially in the case of volunteer firefighters), but to recognize that other motives are at work as well. In addition to being paid to fight fires, it's a safe bet that many firefighters are in that line of work because they are motivated by the danger and excitement associated with the profession, or perhaps the chance to be heroes and to get their pictures in the local paper. Perhaps some firefighters are even motivated by a work schedule that provides significant blocks of time away from the job to pursue other interests. Realistically, most firefighters probably are motivated by a combination of all these things to one degree or another.

Sometimes people help others not because it is their job but because it is expected. For example, adults are expected to help children, and older siblings are expected to help younger siblings. In our society, until recently, men were expected to help women by performing such tasks as opening doors, carrying packages, and walking nearest to the road. Men were trained from a very early age to provide this help, and women were trained to submit to such helpful gestures without question. These things were done routinely by men and women because they were societal expectations. Recently, however, both women and men have begun to examine the motives for these behaviors, and it appears that a decision has been made by many men and women that it perhaps would be best if men and women helped each other, depending on the situation, rather than on the gender.

Numerous other reasons for helping are less laudable than those mentioned thus far. Sometimes people may help because it makes them feel superior to the person or persons receiving their help. Because some people may have the knowledge or skills to do something better than someone else, they might be inclined to feel powerful or special or in some way better than the person who needs the help. By showing someone how much they know or are better able to do something, they can reaffirm their position in the pecking order and put everyone else in his or her place at the same time.

Another not-so-nice reason for helping is to place another person in one's debt. In these instances, people provide help, but with strings attached. The strings come in many forms, but essentially they require the receiver of the help to somehow be willing to pay back the debt that is automatically incurred on accepting assistance. The message implied is, "I will help you now, but you owe me. And you had better not forget that you owe me, because I won't."

The important thing to realize from the discussion so far is that behind every helpful act is a set of motives. These motives are varied in intensity and purpose and are so intermingled that it is difficult to decipher them. Some of these motives are extremely positive; others are equally negative. If we truly are interested in being helpful to those around us, it is vital that we take the time to examine on a regular basis our motives for helping. Perhaps the most important question that any leader can ask himself or herself is, "Why am I doing this?" If you ask yourself this question and you don't like the answer you get, then almost certainly you need to change your behavior or to rearrange your priorities.

Examining one's motives is vital to effective leadership because most human beings are very sensitive to the motives that underlie the actions of others even when these same human beings may not be attuned to the motivational basis for their own behaviors. Most people on the receiving end of help seem to know intrinsically whether the underlying motivation to help is positive or negative. If, on the one hand, they perceive the helper's motives as being essentially negative, they will resist the help that is offered; or, if they are not in a situation to resist (e.g., the flat tire incident), they will accept the help grudgingly and harbor a strong sense of resentment toward the helper. If, on the other hand, they sense the helper's motives as being positive, they not only will accept the help willingly but also will be grateful for the assistance rendered to them.

When Is Help Helpful?

Gibb (1964) suggested two criteria that a particular act of helping must meet if it is to be considered truly helpful. The first criterion is that something must be done better than it was prior to the help being received. The second criterion is that the person receiving the help must become more independent. In other words, the person receiving the help must experience growth as a result of the helping act and have less need in the future to rely on the person who provided the help.

If we apply these criteria to the flat tire examples above, although both strangers changed the tire, neither was truly helpful. The first criterion of helpfulness was clearly met: The task of changing the tire was definitely performed better than you could have performed it because you were unable to change the tire at all. However, the second criterion of helpfulness, which requires that the person receiving the help must become more independent as a result of the helping act, was not met because you were no more prepared to change a tire after the incident than you were before the incident. For the act to have been truly helpful, the person changing the tire would have had to show you step-by-step the procedures for changing a tire, to walk you through the process in detail, so that the next time you had a flat tire, you would know exactly how to solve the problem for yourself.

It is crucial for all educators to realize the importance of the independence criterion as they seek to provide help to their colleagues in the school setting. In the preceding chapter, we stressed that teaching is highly adaptive. In teaching, situations arise that are unique and extremely unpredictable. Satisfactory performance in such an environment requires teachers to carefully assess each situation independently while maintaining the intellectual and technical flexibility needed to design and apply creative solutions.

There are no patented solutions that teachers can memorize and apply in a given situation because in complex human interactions, such as those characterized by teaching, no two situations are ever identical. Too often in the past, teachers have taken a simplistic approach to providing help in solving instructional problems. If a young teacher was experiencing problems in controlling students in the classroom, the best that he or she could look forward to was some sage advice from the principal, who probably had insufficient information or technical expertise to solve the problem in the first place.

In such a situation, the principal might have advised the beleaguered young teacher to put the students in a seating chart, to develop a set of class rules and stick to it doggedly, or not to smile until after Christmas. Maybe the teacher would have been advised to do all of these things simultaneously. But seldom if ever would the teacher be helped by the principal to analyze the problem in detail, isolate the causes, select some plausible solutions, apply those solutions, and then monitor the results and adjust the solutions until a desirable set of classroom conditions was achieved. In other words, the teacher was not *helped* because the teacher was not encouraged to become more independent through gaining an understanding of the process of instructional problem solving.

It is not so surprising that many principals continually complain that some teachers never seem to be able to solve problems in their classrooms and constantly come to them for help. What these principals apparently do not understand is that they have

Increase the Risks			Increase the Benefits
Safety ← Status Quo	← INDIVIDUAL →		Progress → Growth
Decrease the Benefits			Decrease the Risks

Figure 2.1. Factors Determining a Person's Propensity to Seek Risks or Benefits
SOURCE: Adapted from *Toward a Psychology of Being* (p. 47), by A. H. Maslow, 1968, New York: Van Nostrand Reinhold.

never provided any real help to their teachers in the first place because they have not acted in ways that encourage the teachers to grow and to become more independent.

What determines whether or not a person will experience growth when confronted with challenging situations? Maslow (1968) discussed in detail the exciting and equally frightening dilemma associated with choices that human beings make about growth. He noted a conflict between what he termed the "defensive forces" and the "growth trends" that are embedded in the deepest nature of human beings. This conflict can be illustrated in a diagram as shown in Figure 2.1.

The diagram depicts the person as being in the middle, forced to make a choice when confronted with growth situations. Life is essentially a never-ending series of choice situations constantly confronting every individual. Every person must continually "choose between the delights and anxieties of safety and growth, dependence and independence, regression and progression, immaturity and maturity" (Maslow, 1968, p. 47). Safety has both anxieties and delights; growth has both anxieties and delights. People choose growth over safety when they judge the benefits associated with growth as being greater than the dangers or risks associated with that growth. They choose safety when they assess the risks associated with growth as outweighing the benefits associated with growth.

Recently, we were discussing the dilemma associated with choices between growth and safety. An interesting example emerged from our discussion, dating back to our days as preadolescent boys. When we were 13 or 14, we both wanted very much to learn to dance. The truth is that we wanted to learn this skill so that we would be more attractive to girls. We could really enhance our social status with the girls if we learned to dance because few boys at that age were competent dancers, whereas virtually all of the girls were reasonably good dancers. We reasoned that if we could learn to dance, even moderately well, we then could go up to any girl we chose, ask her to dance, and not get rejected.

Although the attractions of learning to dance were great when measured by preadolescent boy standards, the associated risks were also considerable. If we tried to learn to dance simply by dancing at social gatherings, we risked looking foolish in front of our peers. And they would have let us know exactly how foolish we looked! The fear of looking foolish, for most young boys, far outweighed the rewards of being able to dance, so most of us pretended as if we thought dancing was stupid and we didn't want to do it anyway.

If, however, a girl had invited one or two of us over to her home one afternoon to listen to some new records and to learn some dance steps, most of us would have danced at the chance. Why would we have been thrilled to accept an invitation for the private dance lesson? Because the attractions were as strong as ever, but the risks were significantly reduced because only a few people would be present.

Generally, growth occurs in small steps as people interact with their surroundings and gain confidence in themselves. They begin to feel safe enough to take some risks. According to Maslow (1968),

> Assured safety permits higher needs and impulses to emerge and to grow towards mastery. To endanger safety means regression backward to the more basic foundation. What this means is that in the choice between giving up safety or giving up growth, safety will ordinarily win out. Safety needs are prepotent over growth needs. (p. 49)

If teacher leaders are to be truly helpful, they cannot afford to fall into the trap of the principal who dispenses simple remedies for complex problems. They must approach the task of helping teachers in a way that ensures that both of the criteria for helpful behavior are met during the helping act: (a) the task is performed better than it was before the help was extended and (b) as a result of the help, the person receiving the help becomes more independent of the helper. Teacher leaders must strive to enhance the attractions and minimize the dangers associated with growth if teachers are to choose growth over safety in most situations. More is said about this in a later chapter.

The Nature of Human Relationships

Just as there are a variety of motives for helping others, there are also numerous ways of relating to people. Numerous investigations over an extended period have suggested three fundamental dimensions in human relationships: (a) the degree of interpersonal involvement, (b) the exercise of interpersonal control, and (c) the affect or emotional tone of the relationship (Giffen & Patton, 1974). Each dimension is distinct enough to be measured or estimated, and together they can be used to describe almost any human relationship.

Interpersonal involvement refers to the amount of interaction between two people and the importance that each person attaches to this interaction. On the one hand, for example, many people in your life remain on the fringes. Even though you may come into contact with them frequently (e.g., the person who delivers your mail, the clerk at the local supermarket), your relationships with these people remain casual because you never develop any depth of involvement with them. On the other hand, there are other individuals with whom you do not come into contact frequently but with whom you still maintain very deep relationships (e.g., a relative who lives on the opposite side of the country, a very dear friend from college).

The degree of involvement one associates with a relationship is closely related to the personal information one exchanges with others. For a meaningful relationship to exist between two people, each person in the relationship must reveal significant parts of himself or herself to the other person. If neither person chooses to reveal significant personal information to the other, there will be no depth or real involvement in a relationship. If only one person reveals himself or herself to the other, then the relationship will tend to be out of balance.

Suppose, for a moment, that you are a tennis buff, a dedicated enthusiast who really loves to play the game. You love to play so much that you play every morning before going to work. One morning, you arrive at the club, eager to play, only to be disappointed. Your playing partner's wife had called the club and left a message that he is sick and won't be able to play. Before the disappointment can sink in, a young man who happened to be standing at the counter when you got the news about your tennis partner introduces himself as Jeff Granger and asks whether you would like to play tennis with him. You are thrilled at the turn of events and tell him you would be delighted.

As you start to play, you learn some things about Jeff. Although he is a much better player than you, he does not make you feel inadequate. When you hit a good shot, Jeff is free with his compliments. If a ball is close to the line, he gives you the benefit of the doubt. Jeff laughs at your jokes and appears to really enjoy himself.

After the match, you buy Jeff a soda and engage him in conversation while you both relax. You find out he is a college student majoring in special education. His father died when he was 6, and his mother, an elementary school teacher, really has struggled to raise four children alone. You tell him that you are a high school science teacher and that you lost both your parents in an automobile accident when you were 12. You continue to talk and share other personal information. When you are finally ready to leave, you tell Jeff how much you enjoyed the time you spent with him, and he tells you he enjoyed himself as well. At this point, you even may make arrangements to play tennis together again because you sense a pleasant relationship developing. Even if you don't play again, you will most likely share a cordial relationship with Jeff Granger and greet him warmly if you should see him again somewhere.

Just two hours earlier, you didn't know Jeff Granger existed. Because you now have spent some time together and exchanged some personal information, a relationship has been established. How meaningful that relationship will become depends on how much interaction you will have with Jeff in the future and the importance that each of you attaches to that interaction.

Teacher leaders must strive to establish a level of meaningful involvement with all of their teaching colleagues if they hope to be successful in creating helping relationships. It is not sufficient to be involved with other teachers in a superficial manner simply because it is your job and you are expected to do your job. Teacher leaders must take a personal interest in their teaching colleagues that goes beyond seeing them as just teachers, but instead seeks to recognize them as human beings sharing the same human problems, hopes, fears, pain, and joys that all people share.

Once a relationship is established through interpersonal involvement, then the other two dimensions in human relationships —interpersonal control and affect—become significant. *Interpersonal control* refers to who will make the decisions in the relationship and how they will be made. A person who has positive control in a relationship can be referred to in such terms as *dominant, influential, leader, superior,* and *power.* Such terms as *submissive, compliant, follower, subordinate,* and *impotent* can be used to describe a person who lacks interpersonal control in a relationship.

Some people would argue for the existence of a finite amount of power or interpersonal control in any relationship. This power can be distributed between the two parties in a relationship in any proportion (e.g., 50-50, 75-25, or 100-0), depending on the degree to which power is shared. It is vitally important for teacher leaders to understand that the exercise of dominant behavior by one person in a relationship tends to produce submissive responses by the other person in the relationship. The reverse is also true: Submission by one person encourages dominance by the other. In the context of Gibb's second criterion for helpful behavior, it is sometimes necessary for the teacher leader to assume a more submissive posture in working with a particular teacher in order to force the teacher to become more independent in making instructional decisions. At other times, the teacher leader may need to be more directive when dealing with a particular teacher who is going in the wrong direction and cannot seem to realize it.

The power distribution in relationships between teachers and administrators has tended to be rather one-sided in the past. Because of the authority accorded to principals and other administrators by virtue of their formal positions in the organization, teachers have been made to feel essentially powerless in their relationships with administrators. At the same time, the imbalance of power between administrators and teachers has made it difficult, if not impossible in most cases, for administrators and teachers to create helping relationships that allow them to work together collaboratively to solve instructional problems.

Teacher leaders, whether or not they have a formal title such as team leader or department head, must be careful to maintain a healthy balance of power in their relationships with others if they hope to establish collaborative working conditions with their colleagues. Failure to maintain this balance will seriously limit the ability of teacher leaders to create helping relationships.

The third dimension of a relationship—*affect*—is related to the emotional tone of a relationship and involves expressions of warmth, caring, acceptance, and love, as well as expressions of hostility, indifference, rejection, and hate. Affectionate behavior by one person in a relationship tends to produce affectionate responses by the other; hostile behavior by one tends to produce hostility by the other. On the one hand, for example, if you act kindly toward another by praising her or his efforts, that person likely will respond by praising your efforts in return. On the other hand, if you are critical of the efforts of another, that person likely will find fault with your efforts as well. Understanding the reciprocity of expressing positive affect in a relationship has obvious utility for teacher leaders as they work with their colleagues to encourage professional growth. Teacher leaders need to concentrate their energies on creating warm, caring feelings in their relationships with other teachers to establish the level of trust needed to be truly helpful.

Understanding and Using Power

Power is among the most important dynamics operative in both human and organizational contexts. *Power* has been defined as "one person's degree of influence over others to the extent that obedience or conformity follow" (Giammatteo & Giammatteo, 1981, p. 49). Although authority might be considered a broad basis for action not directed at anyone in particular, power is "derived from authority and administratively is directed at winning individual or group compliance" (Sergiovanni & Starratt, 1971, p. 43).

Many people regard power in a negative context. To these people, power connotes dominance and submission, control and acquiescence, the ability of one individual to exert his or her will over the will of another. Most people, however, view power as a necessary condition for leadership, with the exercise of power having both desirable and undesirable expressions. "Power, like any human attribute, can be benevolent or malicious, used or abused, inspiring or stifling, but it is a force within most systems" (Giammatteo & Giammatteo, 1981, p. 48).

Perhaps the most widely recognized typology of the sources of power comes from the writing of French and Raven (1960). They identified five bases of social power that one person can exercise over another: (a) reward power, (b) coercive power, (c) expert power, (d) referent power, and (e) legitimate power.

Reward power stems from the ability to provide others with something they desire in exchange for their compliance with the wishes of the person exercising power. Typical rewards include positive performance evaluations, salary increases, merit bonuses, recognition, special favors, clerical assistance, and favorable work and assignments. *Coercive power* is the opposite of reward power and is exercised by withholding rewards as sanctions for noncompliance with the wishes of the person exercising power. Both of these types of power have been used excessively in the past in the benevolent, paternalistic supervisory environments in schools.

Expert power flows from the ability to gain compliance from others on the basis of knowledge, information, or skills possessed by the person exercising power. Expert power tends to be situational in that the person with the knowledge or skills to deal with a specific set of conditions may be called on to exercise power in a particular situation, but not in another fundamentally different situation. In the flat tire scenarios related earlier in this chapter, the stranger with the expertise to change the tire assumed the power in that particular situation. The person without the expertise that was needed to change the tire had to rely on reward power in the form of a cash payment to gain compliance with his or her wishes.

Referent power is accorded to individuals who are able to command the admiration and respect of others. Those who exercise referent power display certain qualities and characteristics that establish them as role models and cause others to willingly follow them, identify with their goals and objectives, and essentially *trust their motives.* Although referent power frequently is associated with expert power in the sense that one respects and admires a person's competence to perform in a particular role, referent power is conceptually independent of expert power.

Legitimate power refers to an administrative prerogative associated with a formal role in an organization. For example, the principal of a school has legitimate power to direct his or her subordinates in any number of matters. The legitimate power of the principal is a right of office that is legitimated in the organizational structure, as well as in statutes, policies, and administrative guidelines and directives. Subordinates are expected to comply with the legitimate directives of principals and other formally recognized leaders in the school hierarchy. Failure to comply with legitimate directives constitutes insubordination and may bring heavy sanctions.

Very simply, power is the ability to get people to do what you want or need them to do. Few people would argue that teacher leaders need power; the issue is what the bases of that power should be. In reviewing the five sources of power identified by French and Raven, we believe that teacher leaders need to rely on expert and referent power to the maximum extent possible, to use legitimate and reward power only on a limited basis, and to avoid coercive power altogether.

The evidence suggests that expert and referent power seem to provide the strongest correlations with performance and worker satisfaction (Bachman, Bowers, & Marcus, 1968; Bachman, Smith, & Slesinger, 1968). Expert power can be exercised only when one has the competence to expertly perform functions that are essential to the organization. This limitation would suggest that teacher leaders must devote an inordinate amount of time and energy to continually building and refining their knowledge and skills related to teaching and learning. Through sharing their knowledge and skills with teachers, both individually and in group settings, teacher leaders can exercise a strong and constantly growing expert power base.

As mentioned previously, referent power is associated with, but largely independent of, expert power. Teacher leaders can expand their referent power base in several ways. First, teacher leaders must develop a philosophy or system of believing about teaching in particular and education in general that is consistent with the best interests of the students served by the school. This belief system must be refined and communicated effectively to everyone with whom the teacher leader interacts on a regular basis. Actions of the teacher leader in carrying out his or her responsibilities must always be consistent with this established belief system. In this way, over time, an atmosphere of mutual trust and respect based on group acceptance of a teacher leader's beliefs and motives can form the basis for a successful helping relationship among all people working together in the school.

Another important aspect related to establishing a referent power base hinges on the ability of the teacher leader to understand and establish helping relationships. Understanding the nature of human relationships, consistently demonstrating care and respect for others, refining communications skills (especially listening), and examining one's personal motives for exercising power while always seeking to share power with others to the fullest extent possible will surely enhance the referent power of any teacher leader.

Some teachers will have a measure of legitimate power associated with formal job titles, such as curriculum resource teacher, lead teacher, or department head; others will not. For those who have such titles, a set of expectations that generally goes with the job title may even be expressed in a formal job description. It sometimes may be necessary to fall back on legitimate power to accomplish an objective associated with job expectations, such as coordinating a staff development program or conducting a classroom observation, when a particular teacher or group of teachers would prefer not to cooperate. In such situations, it is always better if the task can be accomplished through referent or expert power. If this is not possible, then legitimate power should be used as a last resort because legitimate power is not characteristic of a helping relationship. Each time it is necessary for a teacher leader to use legitimate power to gain compliance from others, the teacher leader's reserve of referent power will be reduced proportionally.

Teacher leaders also need to exercise care when using reward power. The quantity and quality of the rewards available for distribution by teacher leaders will vary from situation to situation. Sometimes teacher leaders will have limited authority over budget allocations or may be in a position to conduct performance reviews or make work assignments. In such instances, it is crucial that whatever rewards are available be distributed on a fair and equitable basis and that the teacher leader not be perceived as using tangible rewards to unduly influence the actions of colleagues.

Coercive power should be avoided by teacher leaders at all costs. The imposition of sanctions has no place in a helping relationship and, if used, will seriously erode the other, more legitimate sources of power available to teacher leaders. If a situation dictates that sanctions must be imposed on a teacher colleague, the teacher leader must recognize that the use of such sanctions is not the responsibility of the teacher leader but of the administration.

The Importance of Sharing Power

In a helping relationship, it is vital that power be shared. Many traditionalists regard power as a finite sum: If you have more, I have less. However, a more enlightened point of view is that power is an expandable pie (Kouzes & Posner, 1990): The more people believe they have power and can influence the organization, the higher job satisfaction and performance will be throughout the organization (Tannenbaum, 1968). When the leader shares power with other people, those people, in turn, have a stake in the performance of the organization and become more committed to helping it succeed through effectively discharging their duties and responsibilities.

> When you strengthen others, your level of influence with them is increased. When you go out of your way on behalf of others, you build up credit with them—credit that may be drawn upon when extraordinary efforts are required. Leaders create a sense of covenant when they help others to grow and develop. When the leader is viewed as helpful, other people will more likely be committed to the leader and the organization's goal. (Kouzes & Posner, 1990, p. 165)

Teacher leaders need to direct their efforts toward building a team spirit in which everyone has an interest in the success or failure of the organization. As power and responsibility are shared with others and as these others respond successfully, they grow as people, and additional power and responsibility can be extended. The appropriate sharing of power will frequently result in a team synergy that far exceeds the capabilities of a collection of individuals to contribute to the good of the organization. The task of the teacher leader is to turn followers into leaders themselves and thereby to expand the potential for productive leadership.

As we noted earlier in this chapter, some people have a negative perception of power, whereas others see power as a positive force for effective leadership. In two ways, people experience and express power needs (McClelland, 1975). One of these ways is essentially negative, a "personalized power concern" or power used to serve oneself. The other way is a "socialized power concern" or power used in the service of others.

A *personalized power concern* generally is directed toward serving the needs of the person exercising power. People with this power orientation are intent on being in the spotlight and collecting the symbols and displaying the trappings of prestige, such as honors and awards, impressive offices, and fancy cars. They also tend to be insensitive to the needs of others and, in fact, are inclined to use other people to advance selfish purposes. A personalized power concern does not encourage the sharing of power with others and can lead to a void in leadership and a breakdown in the effectiveness of the organization when the leader departs.

A person with a *socialized power concern* exercises power for the benefit of others. People with this orientation are emotionally and socially mature. They are less concerned with being widely recognized and are content to use their power to help others grow and succeed. A leader with a socialized power concern cultivates among the group a long-range vision for the organization and is more willing to listen to others and to share power. Because of an orientation toward building commitment to the organization and its long-term goals, this leader is inclined to display a participative coaching style of leadership. When he or she leaves the organization, the impact is lessened because others are in a position to fill the leadership void; their loyalties are to a broader set of organizational goals, rather than restricted to an individual.

Those with a personalized power concern could be equated with Greenleaf's "leader first" type, those who have an unusual power drive to lead in order to acquire material possessions (Greenleaf, 1977). Such individuals may choose to serve others after leadership has been firmly established, but their initial inclination is first to meet personal needs. In contrast with the leader-first leader is the "servant leader," who begins with the need to serve first, then lead. The priority of the servant leader is to make sure the priority needs of others are being met. According to Greenleaf:

> The best test, and difficult to administer, is: Do those served grow as persons? Do they, while being served, become healthier, wiser, freer, more autonomous, more likely themselves to become servants? And what is the effect on the least privileged in society; will they benefit, or, at least, not be further deprived? (pp. 13-14)

The servant leader is first of all a helper, an enabler, one who dedicates himself or herself to the growth and development of others. We believe that, to be successful, teacher leaders should strive to be servant leaders through effectively creating helping relationships. Below is a list of suggested strategies to help them accomplish this purpose.

- Develop an understanding of helping relationships and learn how to be truly helpful to others.
- Constantly assess your motives for helping so that you can effectively build trust relationships with others.
- Work to develop a team attitude that is reflective of a sense of mutual caring and concern.
- Spend significant amounts of time with team members, discussing the organizational mission and working together to develop goals and objectives to accomplish that mission.
- Strive to develop and refine written and oral communications skills.
- Do not be afraid of power; learn to understand and use it wisely.
- Conduct yourself in ways that will make others feel powerful and able to accomplish things on their own.
- Delegate important responsibilities to others with full trust and confidence that they will be met effectively.
- Establish a climate that permits you and encourages others around you to take risks in order to grow.
- Find ways to publicly and privately acknowledge and reward the accomplishments of others on behalf of the organization.
- Learn to follow and receive help, as well as to lead and to give help.

Throughout this chapter, we have emphasized the importance of building helping relationships to providing effective teacher leadership. We briefly described the essential nature of human relationships, what it means to be helpful, the underlying motives for helping, and the uses and misuses of power. We stressed the point that to lead is to serve and that to serve teachers is the foremost responsibility of teacher leaders. In the chapters that follow, we turn our attention to helping teachers better understand the nature of the instructional process, and we offer guidelines to help them as they plan, present, and evaluate lessons for their students.

3

Helping Teachers Make Curriculum Decisions

Few terms associated with education are subject to as much confusion and misunderstanding as *curriculum*. A large part of this problem stems from its many and varied definitions (Zumwalt, 1989). To some educators, curriculum is simply "scope and sequence"; that is, in a particular subject matter, the primary curricular issues are the topics to be covered (scope) and the order in which they should be presented (sequence). To other educators, curriculum is associated with textbooks and other materials (e.g., computer software). This association seems quite reasonable because textbook adoption is often performed by a "curriculum committee." Furthermore, in some classrooms, the curriculum is "defined" by the textbook (or, increasingly, by a computer package; in fact, one very popular company refers to itself as the Computer Curriculum Corporation [CCC]). Still other educators equate curriculum with the design of specific courses. Thus, both determining required and elective courses and preparing course outlines or syllabi are seen as curriculum development activities.

In some more formal definitions, curriculum is contrasted with instruction. Curriculum involves plans; instruction involves action (Pratt, 1980). Curriculum involves the "what"; instruction involves the "how" (Bloom, 1981). Other definitions incorporate instruction within curriculum. Westbury (1989), for example, differentiated the *intended* curriculum from the *implemented* curriculum. He wrote: "The intended curriculum [is] defined as the formal prescribed curriculum contained in national courses of study. The implemented curriculum [is] the curriculum actually taught in the schools" (p. 20). Thus, the intended curriculum more closely resembles Pratt's definition of curriculum, whereas the implemented curriculum is similar to his definition of instruction.

A differentiation also has made between the *manifest* curriculum and the *latent* curriculum (Dreeben, 1968). The manifest curriculum includes the *explicit* aims, goals, and objectives of schools. Literacy and numeracy are important parts of the manifest curriculum of elementary schools. The latent curriculum includes the *implicit* aims, goals, and objectives of schools. Dreeben suggested that order, neatness, and docility are an integral part of the latent curriculum in many schools.

With all these ideas and distinctions floating around, it is small wonder that many teachers find curriculum confusing. To avoid adding to this confusion, we choose to define curriculum as we see it. *Curriculum is the sum total of the experiences that enable students (a) to make sense of what they are being taught in the schools about various academic disciplines and (b) to acquire the knowledge, skills, attitudes, and values believed to be important.* Two aspects of this definition are especially important.

First, curriculum is purposeful. The two major purposes are to help students (a) make sense of the various academic disciplines they encounter and (b) acquire the knowledge, skills, attitudes, and values deemed to be important. Experiences without purpose are omitted from our definition. Students generally do not learn experiences; rather, they learn *from* their experiences.

Second, we define curriculum in terms of what students actually experience, rather than what they are intended to experience. Both planned and unplanned experiences, when related to some purpose, are part of our definition of curriculum. Thus, we err on the side of the implemented curriculum (rather than the intended curriculum) and the latent curriculum (rather than the manifest curriculum). Our decision in this regard was informed by research indicating that, worldwide, the implemented curriculum is generally a better predictor of student achievement than is the intended curriculum (Westbury, 1989).

How the Curriculum
Is Communicated to Students

Students rarely, if ever, see a scope and sequence chart. Although they regularly use textbooks, many of these textbooks do not provide students with a clear understanding of the structure of the subject matter being addressed. Although students complete courses and acquire Carnegie units, they often fail to grasp the rationale behind course requirements or the connections between and among courses (English, 1993). Recently, Galluzo (1994) suggested that many teacher education programs lack focus and are simply "collections of courses which offer no consistent image of what it means to teach, nor what it means to learn to teach" (p. 5956). This same criticism can be made of many of the programs in place in elementary and secondary schools.

If students do not understand curriculum based on the more traditional indicators (e.g., scope and sequence, textbooks, required courses), then how do they come to an understanding? We have two answers to this question. First, students learn about curriculum from the ways teachers, as adults, allocate time to their various studies. Second, during this allocated time, students learn about curriculum by virtue of the tasks teachers assign to them.

Allocated Time

It is noteworthy that Connelly and Clandinin (1993) suggested that "what is called 'curriculum planning' could just as easily be called 'organizing time.' . . . High-minded arguments about the relative importance of particular content topics are often best understood in terms of what to do with limited time. Time, not content, is often the main concern" (p. 9).

Similarly, Anderson (1993) suggested that the way a person allocates time communicates to others what he or she values (i.e., time = values). For example, if learning to use computer technology is important to you, you spend the time necessary to learn how to use it. If you spend time with your family, you communicate to them that they are important. The term *quality time* was quite likely coined by someone who felt guilty that the way he or she spent time did *not* coincide with his or her values.

Differences in educational values are apparent in the way teachers allocate time in both elementary and secondary schools. In elementary schools, approximately three times as much time is spent on reading and language arts as on mathematics (Burns, 1984). Thus, students learn very quickly that literacy is more important than numeracy. They also learn that social studies and science are taught when "there is time." As a consequence, social studies and science are perceived by many students to be at the lower end of the curricular pecking order.

In secondary schools, differences in the amount of time allocated to specific subject matters are minimized by scheduling. Nonetheless, students learn the relative importance of various subject matters by virtue of the required Carnegie units of each. In most high schools, four English units, three mathematics units, two science units, one physical education unit, and no music units are required for graduation. Thus the curricular pecking order learned in elementary school is, once again, reinforced.

In addition to differences in the way time is allocated to the various subject matters are large differences in the amount of time allocated to various topics or skills within the subject matters. In elementary language arts, one teacher may focus on speaking and writing (expressive language), whereas another may emphasize listening and reading (receptive language). In elementary mathematics, the emphasis may be on computational skills, or it may be on problem solving. In a European history course, the emphasis may be on Western Europe, with the entire history of Eastern Europe covered in 2 weeks. Similarly, in a chemistry course, two thirds of the time may be spent on organic (vs. inorganic) chemistry. In all cases, students infer that some topics or skills are more important than others—namely, those to which more time is devoted.

The amount of time allocated to different subject matters typically is determined by state or school district policies. As a consequence, individual teachers have little to say about this issue. Groups of teachers, however, potentially can have a great impact on many of these factors that individual teachers take for granted, a point we return to later.

The amount of time allocated to topics within subject matters, however, is clearly within the purview of individual teachers. In this regard, research suggests that the way a teacher allocates time to various topics depends on three primary factors: (a) the teacher's familiarity with the topic, (b) the perceived difficulty of the topic for the students, and (c) the availability of materials and other resources needed to teach it (Berliner, 1989).

Teachers are more likely to teach topics with which they are familiar. Familiarity likely breeds confidence and ease of planning. Thus, this research finding is easily understood.

Teachers also are more likely to teach the topics they believe students have a good chance of learning than they are to teach those with which students probably will have difficulty. Teachers gain strong psychic rewards from student learning; they are frustrated by nonlearning, particularly when they give it their best shot and the majority of their students still do not learn. Once again, this finding is easily understood.

Finally, teachers are more likely to teach topics for which they have access to the needed materials and resources. If Bunsen burners are not readily available, then many chemistry experiments go unperformed. If a particular video is temporarily unavailable for use, then the topic associated with that video may be postponed or ultimately eliminated.

This discussion is not intended to denigrate teachers for bowing to external pressures in order to make curriculum decisions. Rather, it is intended to suggest that teacher leaders can provide opportunities for teachers to make decisions based on more appropriate concerns. More is said about this issue later in this chapter.

What is to be learned from this discussion of allocated time? Several lessons seem apparent. First, what teachers do is more important than what they say. Teachers may tell students that learning to write is important, but if they spend the equivalent of 10 minutes every other day in writing instruction, students learn that writing is not as important as their teachers say it is. Teachers need to allocate appropriate amounts of time if students are to be convinced of the importance of a particular topic or skill.

Second, some aspects of allocated time are outside the control of individual teachers. If some authority states that 150 minutes per day in elementary schools are to be spent on reading and language arts, individual teachers have no choice but to comply. At the same time, however, teachers collectively have the potential to affect these mandates. They can lobby through their professional associations. They can write letters to their school administrators or their senators and representatives.

Third, some aspects of allocated time individual teachers do control. The decision to skip a chapter in a textbook or to spend 3 weeks on it is a decision made by an individual teacher. The choice to incorporate, rather than omit, the "optional exercises" in a textbook also is a decision made by an individual teacher. An emphasis on memorization of historical events, rather than on understanding of historical issues, is another decision made by an individual teacher. This last example leads us nicely to our next section.

Student Tasks

In addition to the way time is allocated, students come to understand the curriculum by virtue of the tasks they are assigned. A task can be defined in terms of the goal to be achieved and the activities in which the student engages in order to achieve that goal (Doyle, 1979). Thus, tasks incorporate both ends (goals) and means (activities). Consider the following task as an example. Students are expected to gain an appreciation of *Macbeth* by reading the play, watching the movie, and engaging in a discussion with fellow students and the teacher. The first part of this task defines the goal (e.g., gain an appreciation of *Macbeth*). The last two parts indicate the activities (e.g., reading, watching, discussing) that are expected to lead to the attainment of that goal.

The goal inherent in tasks can be defined in terms of either the content (e.g., *Macbeth*) or the process involved in operating on or with that content (e.g., gain an appreciation). Several systems currently exist for classifying both content and process. Anderson and Jones (1981) identified three major content classifications: information, concepts, and procedures. The definitions of these three categories are shown in Table 3.1.

As can be seen in Table 3.1, information contains two subclassifications: facts and opinions. Opinions are somewhat idiosyncratic "knowings"; facts represent consensual "knowledge" (Krathwohl, 1985). That is, facts tend to be supported by evidence or other forms of documentation that enable people to agree on their accuracy or truthfulness. Because information flows fast and furious in most schools, students attend to certain information and ignore other information. By itself, information has no meaning, nor is it useful.

To make sense of information, we form categories that include bits of information that are somehow related; that is, for a bit of information to be placed into a particular category, it must share some thing or things in common with other bits of information in that category. The things it shares are referred to as *essential features* or *critical attributes*. These categories are referred to as *concepts*.

Concepts are the building blocks of understanding. If new information is unrelated to concepts already existing in the mind of the learner, it can be memorized, but it will not be understood. Once concepts have been formed, they can be related to one another. Statements of relationships between or among concepts are called *principles*. The terms *generalizations* and *rules* also are used to refer to relationships among concepts.

To use information, we develop *procedures*. Procedures enable us to translate information into action, either mental or physical. Procedures enable us to perform a sequence of steps to arrive at some desired end. These steps may be a fixed sequence (*linear*) or may require some decision making (*branching*). Procedures may apply to a limited number of situations (*skills*) or to a large variety of settings (*strategies*).

TABLE 3.1   Definitions of Information, Concepts, and Procedures

---

Information can be defined as sentences or phrases that society (or its designates, e.g., curriculum guides, teachers, school boards) believes to be important or interesting in their own right. Two types of information can be identified: facts and opinions. *Facts* represent consensual knowledge. Such knowledge usually is supported by evidence documented in textbooks, reference books, and the like. "Washington, DC, is the capital of the United States" is a fact. *Opinions* represent somewhat more idiosyncratic "knowings." "Washington, DC, is one of the most exciting cities in the United States" is an opinion.

Concepts can be defined as categories of objects, events, experiences, or ideas that give meaning to the symbols we use to communicate (e.g., words, numerals, pictures). All members included in the category must share some thing or things in common. The things they share are termed the *critical attributes* or *defining features*. Relationships among concepts are referred to as *principles*. In mathematics, for example, *area, rectangle, equals, length, multiply,* and *width* are all concepts. The formula $A = l \times w$ is a principle. Principles sometimes are referred to as *generalizations* or *rules*.

Procedures can be defined as sequences of mental or physical activities that can be used to solve problems, gather information, or achieve some desired goal. Two types of procedures are of interest in most school settings. *Linear procedures* are those in which the sequence of activities is performed in order; that is, regardless of the outcome of the first activity, the second activity is performed on the basis of that outcome. *Branching procedures* are those in which one or more of the activities involve decision making; that is, depending on the outcome of the first activity, the person may need to perform either the second or the third activity. Procedures that apply to a limited, finite set of situations are called *skills*. Many of these procedures are linear. Finally, procedures that apply to an extended, indefinite set of situations are called *strategies*. Most of these procedures are branching.

SOURCE: Adapted from "Designing Instructional Strategies to Facilitate Learning for Mastery," by L. W. Anderson and B. F. Jones, 1981, *Instructional Psychologist, 16,* p. 127.

The importance of these classifications in curriculum stems from the fact that academic disciplines can be structured differently by emphasizing different content categories. Mathematics can be taught as a set of facts to be memorized (e.g., multiplication tables, the Pythagorean theorem). Mathematics also can be taught as a set of concepts to be understood and related to one another (e.g., quadrilateral, polygon; equations, formulas). Finally, mathematics can be taught as a set of procedures (algorithms) to be applied to a variety of routine and nonroutine problems (e.g., the procedures for solving a quadratic equation, the techniques for solving simultaneous equations). Finally, mathematics can be taught as some combination of the above.

Similarly, history can be taught as a set of "great men and big events" (e.g., Napoleon, the signing of the Magna Carta). History can be taught as a set of concepts (e.g., conflicts, treaties, international law). History also can be taught as a set of procedures (e.g., differentiating fact from opinion, developing a logical argument). And, once again, history can be taught on balance.

The way a teacher structures a discipline provides students with their understanding of that discipline. Thus, first-grade children who are given a steady diet of sound-symbol relation tasks (e.g., the letter *a* having different sounds) gain a very different understanding of what reading means from those who learn to read within the context of stories (e.g., *The Cat in the Hat*). Saying the words properly is quite different from gaining meaning from the printed page.

Arguably, the best-known system for classifying the mental operations inherent in the tasks we assign students is Bloom's (1956) taxonomy of educational objectives. The five levels of the taxonomy, brief descriptions of each level, and verbs indicative of the level of thinking required at each level are shown in Table 3.2. Also included in Table 3.2 are sample questions that may be asked of students about the story of Goldilocks and the three bears to determine whether they have achieved each of these five levels.

Some educators have found the individual levels of the taxonomy to be somewhat problematic (Anderson & Sosniak, 1994). Several of these educators have suggested reducing the taxonomy to two levels: lower order and higher order. Generally speaking, lower order implies memory, whereas higher order implies that the student is able to go "beyond memory" or "beyond the informa-

TABLE 3.2 Bloom's Taxonomy of Cognitive Objectives: Definitions, Key Words, and Examples (From the story "Goldilocks and the Three Bears")

Evaluation:	Judging [the worth of] material, ideas, and problems based on established criteria [either explicit or implicit]
Key Words:	*Debate, defend, evaluate, judge, justify*
Example:	Was Goldilocks good or bad? Why do you think so?
Synthesis:	Producing a solution by using original, creative thinking [based on analytical relationships]
Key Words:	*Compose, create, design, formulate, imagine*
Example:	How might the story have been different if Goldilocks had visited the three *fishes* instead of the three bears?
Analysis:	Breaking down the given material into its constituent parts and seeing relationships [among the parts]
Key Words:	*Analyze, distinguish, relate, separate*
Example:	What parts of the story could not really have happened?
Application:	Using what has been learned [in a novel situation] to solve a problem
Key Words:	*Apply, demonstrate, determine, show, use*
Example:	If Goldilocks had come to your home, what might she have eaten (instead of porridge)?
Comprehension:	Showing that the meaning has been understood
Key Words:	*Explain, illustrate, interpret, rephrase, translate*
Example:	Why did Goldilocks like the things that belonged to the baby bear?

tion given" (Bruner, 1979). This rather simple distinction between memory and "beyond memory" can be quite useful for those involved in curriculum decisions.

When the three content classifications mentioned earlier are combined with the two major taxonomic classifications, a six-cell table like that in Table 3.3 can be constructed. As shown in Table 3.3,

TABLE 3.3 A Content × Mental Process Matrix

Mental Process

Content	*Lower order*	*Higher order*
Information Facts Opinions		
Concepts Principles		
Procedures Linear Branching Skills Strategies		

information can be memorized or acted on by using "higher mental processes." Similar statements can be made for concepts and procedures.

Table 3.3, then, can serve as a heuristic for teachers interested in conducting a critical examination of a curriculum within a school, a particular subject matter within a school, or a specific course within a subject matter. This examination begins by selecting a sample of the tasks routinely assigned to students (e.g., textbook and workbook exercises, projects, test items). Each task is placed into one or more of the cells of the table. Row and column totals can be computed, and the relative proportion of tasks in each cell can be calculated.

Even a cursory examination of the table will indicate the degree of balance evident in the curriculum. In this regard, we agree with Sanders (1966) that the best curriculum is one that produces a "varied intellectual atmosphere in a classroom" (p. 2).

What can be learned from this discussion of tasks? First, tasks are a primary vehicle for communicating to students the meaning of a curriculum. Thus, care must be taken in selecting the most appropriate learning tasks for students. Second, tasks contain both goals and activities. It is critical that tasks be designed so that activities will likely lead to goal accomplishment; that is, students need to understand that if they engage in the activities of a task, their chances of achieving the goal are quite good. Third, the goals inherent in tasks can be examined in terms of content and processes. Focusing on both of these elements will enable teachers to influence the structure of the curriculum as seen by students and to design curricula that are balanced and varied in terms of the tasks assigned to students.

Recurrent Curricular Problems

Many of the major problems confronting educators are curricular in nature. Bruner (1960) stated this point quite clearly more than three decades ago when he wrote:

> It is quite plain, I think, that the task of improving American schools is not simply one of technique—however comforting it would be to some professional educators to think so. What is at issue, rather, is a deeper problem, one that is more philosophical than psychological or technological in scope. Let me put it in all innocence. What do we conceive to be the end product of our educational effort? I cannot help but feel that this rather overly simplified question has become obscured. (p. 191)

In this section, we address four curricular problems, the solutions to which we believe are central to quality education and school improvement: (a) time constraints, (b) activity-focused learning experiences, (c) teacher autonomy, and (d) lack of resources.

Time Constraints

Students attend school approximately 180 days per year. They typically are in school at least 6 hours each day. Thus, in any given year, students have slightly more than 1,000 hours to learn what they are supposed to learn. At one point in educational history, this amount of time was probably sufficient. However, with the increased amount of information that has accrued over the past several decades and the increased complexity of the skills and strategies that are required to survive, let alone prosper, in the modern world, one must question whether 1,000 hours per year is sufficient.

Most people would answer this question in the negative. Given a negative answer, educators have two choices. First, they can increase the amount of time students spend in school. This is the approach favored by proponents of year-round education (Ballinger, 1993). Second, they can decrease the amount of content and/or the number of goals they expect students to learn during the available time. This choice is consistent with the principles underlying mastery learning (Guskey, 1994) and the Coalition of Essential Schools (Sizer, 1984).

Until policy changes are made in the amount of time allocated to schooling, however, there really is only one option: Educators need to reduce what they expect students to learn and focus on the essentials. They certainly cannot continue to increase the knowledge and skills they expect students to acquire during the same time frame that was in place almost a century ago.

The fundamental curriculum question then becomes, What's worth learning? We believe three principles to be important in answering this question. First, concepts and their relationships are the fundamental building blocks of subject matter understanding. The various number systems and operations define the structure of arithmetic. The periodic table of the elements helps students conceptualize chemistry. Character, plot, setting, and related concepts are central to an understanding of literature. Thus, tasks involving concepts are critical for all subject matter at all age levels.

Second, strategies permit students to generalize what they have learned and to become lifelong learners. Students should be taught a whole host of important strategies: memorization strategies, information-gathering strategies (e.g., observation, using reference materials), organizational strategies (e.g., outlining, note taking), and problem-solving strategies (cf. Polya, 1960). Strategies do not replace content; rather, they permit students to learn content for themselves. Thus tasks including strategies are essential in all curricula.

Third, facts are transient; they are quickly learned and just as quickly forgotten. Furthermore, as time goes by, many facts become obsolete. New evidence replaces old evidence. Centuries ago, the fact that the sun revolves around the earth was replaced by the fact that the earth revolves around the sun. New agreements replace old agreements. What was formerly the country of Yugoslavia is now four separate countries, each with its own capital city. Time spent on facts, then, is often time wasted. The only exception to this statement that we would make concerns those facts that must be recalled and used frequently (e.g., the alphabet, multiplication tables, chemical formulas). Stated somewhat differently, facts that are more easily remembered than looked up in books and other materials should be taught. In general, however, tasks oriented toward facts should be few in number and carefully chosen.

Once the primary tasks have been identified, the time needed to help students achieve them must be estimated. Cook (1971) developed a rather simple procedure for calculating the amount of time needed for completion of a task. This procedure is outlined in Table 3.4.

As can be seen in Table 3.4, our hypothetical teacher would need to allocate at least 7.5 hours to this unit. Taking into consideration all things that could go wrong, however, this teacher could spend as many as 17.5 hours on it. Thus, both the teacher and his or her students would be better served if 12.5 hours were allocated to the unit.

If, after identifying the most important tasks for any particular curricular unit, the estimated allocated time still exceeds the amount of time available, additional reductions would be needed. These reductions should be made within the context of larger curricular units, perhaps even years of study. For example, some tasks may be common across several grade levels of the elementary school science curriculum. Emphasizing these tasks during 2 or 3 years, rather than including them every year, may result in substantial time savings overall.

TABLE 3.4 A Procedure for Estimating the Time
Needed to Accomplish Tasks

Step Number	Description
1	Identify the major tasks to be included in a particular curricular unit (e.g., course, semester, marking period).
2	For each task, estimate the expected time (E) it will take under normal circumstances for most students to achieve the task.
3	For each task, estimate the pessimistic time (P). This is the time it will take if everything that conceivably could go wrong does so.
4	Calculate the average of these two estimates $(E + P)/2$. This is the amount of time to be allocated to the task.

Example:

A teacher is planning a unit that has four tasks. Calculations are as follows (all figures are in hours).

Task	Expected Time	Pessimistic Time	Allocated Time
A	1	3	2
B	3	7	5
C	1.5	2.5	2
D	2	5	3.5
Total	7.5	17.5	12.5

Activity-Focused Learning Experiences

Few educators can doubt that typical classrooms are characterized by a great deal of activity. Researchers have documented more than 1,000 interchanges (e.g., questions, answers, directions, explanations) between elementary teachers and their students in the course of a full day of teaching (Jackson, 1968). During a given semester, students participate in lectures, demonstrations, recitations, discussions, group work, seatwork, reports, contests and games, laboratory exercises, tutorials, and tests (Stodolsky, 1988). Clearly, students are busy. But are they productive?

The distinction between being busy and being productive is central to understanding curriculum. It is a rather simple distinction. We all know people who work very hard but who accomplish very little. Even elementary school students differentiate between "busy work" and activities that are beneficial (Anderson, 1993). Ask a child what he or she *did* during a given school day, and you most likely will get a litany of activities. Ask the same child what he or she *learned* during that same school day, and the most frequent response is "Nothing."

Within our definition of curriculum (mentioned earlier), classroom activities must have a purpose, and this purpose must be made clear to students. There are many reasons for asking students to prepare book reports. A teacher may wish to ensure that students have read assigned books. A teacher may wish to understand students' impressions of a particular book. A teacher may wish to know the extent to which students are able to read critically. These are all legitimate reasons. The issues become (a) what the real reason for the activity is and (b) whether the students understand it.

As mentioned earlier, tasks link activities with purpose. Thus, thinking about the curriculum in terms of tasks is a useful first step in eliminating activity-focused learning environments. Tasks can be derived in two ways. In the first way, consistent with the Tyler rationale (Tyler, 1949), teachers can specify the goal or objective to be achieved and *then* determine the activities in which students should engage to achieve it. Evidence is ample, however, that many teachers do not follow this prescribed sequence of events (Clark & Peterson, 1986). Thus a second way of operationalizing tasks is both necessary and appropriate. Teachers can decide on their classroom activities and *then* ask themselves, What are the purposes of these activities? What do I expect my students to learn as a result of engaging in these activities?

In answering these questions, teachers need to be honest with themselves. Several years ago, one of us (Anderson) took part in a national study of Chapter I programs and classrooms (Rowan & Guthrie, 1989). One teacher made extensive use of mathematics worksheets, many of which seemed excessively long. Initial questions about the length of the worksheets were responded to in terms of the students' need for a great deal of practice. On subsequent questioning, however, the teacher admitted that she did not want any student to complete the worksheets during the class period and then have nothing to do. Thus, a second purpose emerged: classroom management.

Although activities may have multiple purposes, each activity should have at least one. The identification and communication of purpose is necessary for productive learning to occur.

Teacher Autonomy

Teacher autonomy is a two-edged sword. As Anderson (1987a) wrote, "Teacher autonomy is neither 'good' nor 'bad.' Unbridled, it becomes license; excessively controlled, it becomes standardized; and somewhere in between, it provides the freedom needed by teachers to function professionally and effectively in their classrooms" (p. 368). Thus, the problem as Shulman (1983) saw it is to "find a way to make teaching and systems of education both responsible and free" (p. 503).

To achieve this balance between responsibility and freedom, it is necessary to differentiate those conditions or situations in which autonomy is advisable and, in fact, essential and those in which autonomy is ill-advised and potentially problematic. Two primary areas provide useful starting points: curricular content and teaching strategies.

Schwille et al. (1983) differentiated between authority over curricular content and control over teaching strategies. Although they argued that their study was "value free" in terms of the autonomy issue, they clearly implied that the control of curricular content should lie beyond the individual teacher if the continuity and consistency needed to sustain an educational system are to be ensured. Thus, although individual teacher control of teaching strategies is desirable, the relinquishing of individual teacher control of content is necessary if student learning over the long term is to be optimized.

Ryan (1983), however, argued that, with regard to teaching strategies, there are times when teacher freedom needs to be bridled. Specifically, teachers need *more autonomy* in deciding how to reach an objective when successful attainment of that objective is highly *unpredictable* (when the linkage between the performance of activities and goal attainment is tenuous). In contrast, teachers need *less autonomy* in deciding how to reach a goal when successful goal attainment is highly *predictable* (when the performance of the activities will virtually guarantee that the goal will be attained).

In many ways, the key to understanding teacher autonomy is to differentiate between *teacher* as an individual noun and *teacher* as a collective noun. Somewhat paradoxically, it is only when individual teachers are willing to surrender some of their autonomy that teachers collectively will secure the autonomy they need to function as professionals. Quite clearly, teacher leaders have a large role to play in replacing idiosyncratic teacher concerns and opinions with more consensual ones.

Lack of Resources

Many, if not most, classroom activities require materials. Although educators in the United States take this statement for granted, the impact of the availability (and, often, unavailability) of materials on classroom activities is quite clear in research conducted in developing countries (Farrell, 1989). The provision of textbooks to all students enables teachers to assign the reading of a chapter to one group of students while working with another group. Without textbooks, this activity would be virtually impossible. In the United States, the learning of science may be limited by the availability of laboratory equipment, the learning of calculus may be inhibited by the lack of graphic calculators, and learning to write may be hindered by insufficient word processing capabilities.

We are not suggesting that teachers engage in fund-raising activities so that they can secure all of the equipment and materials they need to support their teaching. We are suggesting, however, that teachers engage in joint development of curricular materials and the sharing of materials. Part of this sharing involves critiques of available materials so that inadequate materials are neither purchased nor used.

Teacher Leadership for
Curriculum Decision Making

What can teacher leaders do in terms of curriculum decision making? Three major activities come immediately to mind.

Create a Sense of Urgency Related to Curricular Issues

Echoing Bruner's (1960) sentiments, educators for too long have believed that our educational ills can be cured with technical and technological solutions. Better-prepared teachers, smarter students, more-involved parents, smaller class sizes, increased technology—these all have been perceived to be the keys to educational excellence. It is time educators realize that they may not be. Rather, the keys may reside in community values and how these values are communicated to the children. Values lie at the heart of all discussions on curriculum. Teachers need to lead these critical discussions.

Teacher leaders can design and implement a series of curriculum seminars. Topics for these seminars can include the following:

- What is our professional knowledge base? What truths do we hold to be self-evident? What knowledge should we as teachers share?
- What is worth learning? Should all students learn the same things? Would you endorse a core curriculum? If there are different curricular tracks, how should/do they differ? Do they differ in terms of topics taught, complexity of material, standards used to judge the quality of learning?
- How much autonomy should individual teachers have? In what areas is individual teacher autonomy important? In what areas is individual teacher autonomy unwarranted?

In addition, teacher leaders can be involved in the preparation of a series of short, informative pieces on important curricular matters. These pieces, either written or video, can be circulated within particular schools or districts, incorporated into current

TABLE 3.5 Steps Toward a Curriculum Audit

Step Number	Description
1	Develop an ongoing auditing plan, perhaps over a 4- or 5-year period. The organizational framework for the plan can be either subject area or grade (or other) level.
2	Each year, appoint a group of auditors. The group should consist of a minimum of three teachers, one school administrator, and one "outside" person.
3	Randomly select 50 to 100 tasks for each course included in that year's audit.
4	Analyze the tasks in terms of Tables 3.3 and 3.4.
5	Compare the results of the analysis across all courses included in the audit.
6	Prepare and circulate a report of the findings, complete with recommendations.

district or school publications (e.g., newsletters), or submitted for distribution through various professional associations. Regardless of the vehicle, teachers collectively must make known their positions on critical curricular issues.

Engage in a Curriculum Audit

A *curriculum audit,* in essence, is an examination of time and tasks. Six steps that can be followed in conducting a curriculum audit are shown in Table 3.5.

As can be seen in Table 3.5, the audit begins with a 4- or 5-year auditing plan. For each of these years, a different subject matter or level (grade or other) is identified for auditing purposes. In elementary schools, for example, the first year may focus on prekindergarten (or child development), kindergarten, and first grade. In secondary schools, the first year may focus on science or on introductory levels in all subject areas.

Once the subject matter or level has been identified, an auditing team is appointed. These appointments can be made by the school principal, the administrative council, the school leadership team, or another person or group. The auditing team should consist of three teachers, one school administrator, and one "outside" person. The outside person can be a member of the school district office staff, a representative from a nearby college or university, or a qualified parent (e.g., president of the PTA or PTO).

The first task of this auditing team is to determine all of the courses (e.g., third-grade reading/language arts, Algebra I) that fall within its jurisdiction. The second task is to meet briefly with all of the teachers involved with these courses and to lay out the master plan for the year. The teachers should be told that (a) 50 to 100 tasks will be selected from each course for analysis; (b) the analysis will be based on content, process, and time (e.g., Tables 3.3 and 3.4); (c) a cross-course analysis also will be conducted; and (d) teachers will have opportunities to read and react to drafts of the report before the final report is prepared and circulated.

Curriculum audits have a number of benefits, two of which are worthy of mention. First, for many teachers, curriculum audits permit them to truly "see" their curriculum for the first time. More precisely, they begin to look at the curriculum from a student's point of view. Because the concept of task is embedded in a curriculum audit, teachers begin to look beyond the classroom activities and beyond the textbooks. Because time is an integral part of a curriculum audit, teachers become more pragmatic in their curricular considerations.

Second, curriculum audits provide a common framework for talking about and making informed decisions about curriculum. Any type of common framework moves teachers away from idiosyncratic thoughts, beliefs, and feelings into a more consensually based, professional way of making decisions. Furthermore, the cross-course analysis permits teachers to move beyond conceptions of curriculum as course- or subject-specific to a view of curriculum that permits and even encourages interdisciplinary teaching, multi-age grouping, and similar approaches.

The major deterrent to curriculum audits is the time they take. The approach suggested in Table 3.5, however, minimizes the time needed in two ways. First, not all subject matters or levels are audited at the same time; this would be an overwhelming task. Second, a sample of tasks is selected from each identified course. The selection of a sample, rather than a reliance on the total population, makes the audit doable. If money can be found to employ the auditing team in the summer, it would be wise to relegate Steps 5 and 6 to the summer. Both of these steps require fairly large blocks of time, which typically are not available to working teachers.

Work Toward Developing a
Shared, Quality Set of Materials

A final curricular activity in which teacher leaders can engage is the development and maintenance of a quality set of materials to which all teachers have access. Unfortunately, at the present time, little in the way of systematic evaluation of curriculum materials exists. Teacher leaders can work toward the evaluation of materials; the brief questionnaire shown in Table 3.6 provides a basis for such an evaluation.

This questionnaire is intended to be used as follows. Each teacher would have several copies. Shortly after using a particular material or set of materials in class (e.g., a book chapter, a worksheet, a piece of computer software), the teacher would take a few moments to complete the questionnaire. Completed questionnaires would be given to some designated individual and stored in a central location. Many school districts have developed teacher centers or curriculum centers; such a location would be ideal for storage of these questionnaires.

Periodically, the completed questionnaires would be reviewed, and materials receiving consistently low ratings would be noted. Teachers would be made aware of these materials by posting notices on bulletin boards (including electronic bulletin boards) and/or including them in newsletters. In this way, inferior materials would be regularly eliminated from the curriculum.

TABLE 3.6 Questionnaire for Reviewing Curriculum Materials

Directions: Complete as soon as possible after using the material.
For Questions 1-5, 7, and 8, circle your responses. For Question 6,
write in your response and indicate whether the number refers to
hours or minutes. Before responding to the questions, however,
please provide the information requested in the next section.

A. "Title" of material _____

B. Brief description _____

C. Subject matter _____ Level _____

D. Questionnaire completed by _____

Question	*Response*
1. Is this material acceptable in terms of school and community values?	Yes No ? NA
2. Is treatment of minorities, women, religion, and politics accurate, balanced, and valid?	Yes No ? NA
3. Is this material appropriate for the students, the teachers, the program, and the school?	Yes No ? NA
4. Does this material actively involve students?	Yes No ? NA
5. Is this material effective in helping students achieve the intended goal or objective? (Please describe briefly the objective.)	Yes No ? NA
_____	
_____	
_____	
6. How much time does this material require of students to complete it? _____	
7. Is this material accurate, realistic, and up-to-date?	Yes No ? NA
8. Is the physical quality of this material (e.g., legibility, color) good and uniform?	Yes No ? NA

SOURCE: Adapted from *Curriculum: Design and Development* (p. 395), by
D. Pratt, 1980, Orlando, FL: Harcourt Brace Jovanovich.

Ultimately, those materials receiving consistently high ratings would be noted. Files including the "title" of the material, a brief description, the subject matter, level, and average ratings would be prepared and maintained. Files in a computerized database would be the most appropriate method of doing this.

As in the case of all curriculum development or curriculum evaluation activities, the elimination of inferior materials and the cataloging of quality materials are time-consuming. If possible, some person or persons should be provided with a reduced class load to perform these activities. The benefits of these activities are obvious. Furthermore, with the proliferation of increasing varieties of curriculum materials, such activities are becoming even more important.

Closing Comment

Earlier in this chapter, we suggested that people spend time on what they value. It follows that if educators value curriculum development and evaluation, they will spend time on it. Unfortunately, too many teachers have too little time to spend on these activities. They are too busy teaching too many class periods with too many students. Thus, they cannot *find* time to work on curricular issues. We agree that it is difficult to find time. We would suggest, however, that teachers must *make* time to do so.

Spreading the workload around is one way of ensuring that teachers spend at least some time on curriculum development and evaluation. Few teachers would object to spending 2 hours per month on such activities. Teacher leaders can help organize curriculum work so that the monthly demands on teachers are minimum but the concerted effort of the entire faculty pays off great dividends.

Securing external funds to support summer curriculum development is a means of buying time. Summers provide blocks of time that are sorely needed for meaningful discussion and deliberation of curricular issues. Summers also provide unique opportunities for teachers to work together in groups for a common good. Teacher leaders can write and submit grants intended to secure the necessary funding.

Unlike teaching, which is public, most curriculum work is private. Thus, unlike teaching, curriculum work often "comes out of a teacher's hide." Teacher leaders must work toward increasing the prominence and importance of curriculum work. As Abraham Lincoln once said, "Perhaps if we knew what we were about, we could go about it better."

PART TWO

The Instructional Process

4

Helping Teachers
Plan Instruction

The importance of careful planning has long been recognized in many fields, including education. The 1992 edition of Bartlett's *Familiar Quotations* contains more than 20 sayings about planning. The majority of these pertain to the pitfalls associated with *not* planning. Among these, "To fail to plan is to plan to fail" is perhaps the most famous. Difficulties caused by a lack of planning are also evident in the well-recognized sign:

For teachers, planning produces something of a paradox. On the one hand, most understand the importance of planning; on the other hand, virtually all have very little time to engage in it. Thus, using the equation formulated in the previous chapter (time = values), one might conclude that teachers do not value planning. Such a conclusion would most assuredly be false.

Elementary school teachers traditionally have no planning periods built into the school day. They work with their students from the time they arrive at 8:30 A.M. until they leave at 3:00 P.M. If they are not directly teaching these students, they are engaged in bus duty, hall monitoring, or recess supervision. Thus, when they plan (as all must do), they do so on their own time.

Secondary school teachers may have a single planning period during the school day. During this period, however, they typically must plan for a variety of courses and/or students. Furthermore, because they may be responsible for as many as 200 students, this planning period more likely may be spent grading papers, rather than planning the next day's activities.

The two major issues surrounding teacher planning, then, concern (a) finding the time needed for planning and (b) helping teachers become more effective and efficient in their planning efforts. Both of these issues are addressed in this chapter. Before recommendations are made on these issues, however, a brief discussion of the meaning of planning and a description of what is known about teacher planning seems in order.

Teacher Planning: A Definition

Teacher planning has two definitions. The more pragmatic of the two suggests that planning is what people do when they plan; that is, people formulate plans, and this formulation itself defines planning. In contrast, the more psychological of these two definitions suggests that planning is a process by which a person *visualizes* the future and *creates a framework* to guide his or her actions in that future. Within the context of this chapter, the second definition appears far more appropriate.

Two aspects of this second definition are noteworthy. First, planning involves visualization; that is, as they plan, teachers are guided equally by a sense of what *is possible* and a realization of what *is*. Thus, although teachers are acutely aware of their goals, they also are cognizant of the resources at their disposal that may facilitate or inhibit goal attainment.

Second, planning creates a process or procedure by which one moves toward the attainment of the goals. Thus, planning moves the *possible* into the *likely*. More specifically, planning involves determining a series or sequence of steps that must be carried out if the vision is to be realized and if the goals explicit or implicit in the vision are to be attained. These steps, quite obviously, take into consideration the context in which the plan is to be actualized and the constraints the planner is likely to encounter as the steps are implemented.

Now that planning has been defined, it can be thought about in several ways (Yinger, 1994). First, one may think about planning from a *technical* perspective. From this perspective, the *form* of the plan is central. In other words, how the plan looks is more important than what it represents substantively. If a plan is supposed to include objectives, activities, and assessments, a "good" plan includes all three elements. The nature, quality, and appropriateness of the objectives, activities, and assessments are not issues from a purely technical point of view.

Second, one may think of planning from a *psychological* perspective; that is, teachers may examine their plans, not in terms of the form they take, but in terms of what students are expected to do (the *activities*), the *content* they need in order to do it, and what they are to learn from doing it (the *objectives*). This perspective means that teachers focus more on the substance of the plans than on their form.

Finally, one may conceptualize planning from an *ecological* point of view; that is, one may focus on the connection between planning and action, between vision and reality. Within this context, our emphasis is not on what is on paper (or in the minds of teachers), but what actually transpires in classrooms.

The technical perspective is both efficient and *in*effective; that is, planning from a technical perspective is efficient for those who need to make judgments about plans with little time to do so. Many school principals, for example, confronted with the task of reviewing the lesson plans of many teachers during a short time period, endorse the technical point of view out of necessity.

In contrast, the technical perspective is ineffective for two reasons. First, as mentioned earlier, it emphasizes form over substance; that is, a technical review of plans tends to be quite superficial. Ironically, it is this superficiality that leads to the efficiency of this perspective. Second, those operating from a purely technical point of view often fail to consider the connection between planning and action. If the plans "look good," it makes no difference whether they are feasible or, once in classrooms, teachers act in accordance with their plans.

Having rejected the technical perspective, our approach to planning lies somewhere between the psychological and ecological points of view; that is, we believe that plans must be examined from the students', as well as the teachers', viewpoints. In addition, educators also need to consider how teachers' visions are translated into realities. When planning is looked at in this manner, the likelihood of developing effective plans is increased.

What Is Known About Teacher Planning?

During the past several decades, much has been learned about why teachers plan, the length of time for which they plan, and how they plan. Each of these issues is discussed in this section.

Why Teachers Plan

Teachers plan for several reasons (Clark & Peterson, 1986). Some plan in order to reduce anxiety and uncertainty. Such teachers have difficulty operating from a "seat of the pants" mentality. They prefer knowing what they intend to do and what options they have if their plans do not go according to schedule. Others plan in order to give direction and structure to their teaching. These teachers plan in order to have access to needed resources (e.g., tape recorders, computers). They also plan so that the classroom activities in which they engage students are likely to lead to intended goals or outcomes.

Finally, teachers plan in order to satisfy administrative requirements. They are told to hand in lesson plans on a weekly basis. They do so. They are required to develop course syllabi and to make them available to administrators, as well as to students.

They do so. To fully understand planning and plans, teacher leaders must understand which of these reasons—reducing anxiety, satisfying a need for direction or structure, or fulfilling an administrative requirement—lies at the heart of teacher planning.

Length of Time for Which Teachers Plan

Teachers' plans may reflect a variety of lengths of time: quarterly (or grading period) plans, weekly plans, and daily plans. We refer to these as *temporal* plans. In addition, teacher plans may reflect the nature of the subject matter or courses being taught: course plans (e.g., syllabi), unit (e.g., "book chapter") plans, and lesson plans. We term these *substantive* plans.

Quite clearly, there is a correspondence between temporal and substantive plans. Lesson plans generally are for 1 day. Units require more time to complete (e.g., weeks, sometimes quarters). Finally, courses typically last 1 year. Some of this correspondence, however, is artificially imposed. Lessons certainly may last for more than 1 day. Grading periods, in fact, may end in the middle of units. Multiyear courses do exist (e.g., algebra).

Unfortunately, temporal planning usually takes precedence over substantive planning. Lessons can last only 1 day. Grades must be given whether or not a unit is completed. Multiyear courses are divided into "subcourses" (e.g., Algebra I, Algebra II). Because substantive plans are likely to reflect psychological and ecological concerns, whereas temporal plans tend to reflect technical concerns, we support substantive planning; that is, we need to think about planning in terms of subject matter issues, rather than arbitrary time constraints. At the same time, however, we realize that teachers must operate within a variety of constraints, time included.

How Teachers Plan

Quite obviously, not all teachers plan in the same way. Teachers differ in their views of planning and the starting points of their planning. Teacher planning also changes as teachers move from being novices to being experts.

Incremental Versus Comprehensive Planners. In common terminology, incremental planners focus on the trees, whereas comprehensive planners see the forest. Incremental planners emphasize the details, whereas comprehensive planners highlight the big picture. Temporally speaking, incremental planners may produce a wonderful set of lessons plans that lead nowhere. In contrast, comprehensive planners may develop excellent course syllabi but have no idea of the smaller units of planning that are needed to implement the syllabi successfully.

A balanced view of planning is most beneficial; that is, aspects of both comprehensive and incremental planning are essential to "good" planning. Comprehensive planning provides the overall context within which incremental planning can be effective. Similarly, incremental planning focuses attention on the daily operational issues that must be addressed if comprehensive plans are to be implemented successfully.

Child-Oriented Versus Subject-Oriented Planners. Historically, a distinction has been made between child-oriented teachers and subject-oriented teachers (Cuban, 1984a). In this regard, elementary school teachers generally are regarded as more child oriented, whereas secondary school teachers are seen as more subject oriented. The fact is that both sets of teachers teach children *and* subjects. Perhaps a more appropriate way of understanding this difference, however, is as temporal; that is, some teachers are more present oriented, whereas others are more future oriented. Present-oriented teachers begin their planning with where students are and then decide on how to get them to where they want them to be. In contrast, future-oriented teachers begin their planning with where they want students to be and then decide on how to get them there.

A bridge analogy is useful in understanding these two very different points of view (see Figure 4.1). At the left end of the bridge are the entry characteristics of students—the knowledge, skills, attitudes, and values students bring to the classroom (Bloom, 1976). At the right end are the desired exit characteristics—the knowledge, skills, attitudes, and values teachers hope students

WHERE STUDENTS ARE   WHERE WE WANT
                                      STUDENTS TO BE

Figure 4.1. Planning as "Bridge Building"

will possess when they leave the classroom. The issue, simply put, is whether teachers should build the bridge from left to right (present-oriented teachers) or from right to left (future-oriented teachers). The dangers of beginning at either end are evident. On the one hand, if teachers begin on the left, they may never get to the right; that is, if they begin where students are, they may never get them to where they want them to be. On the other hand, if teachers begin where they want students to be (the right-hand side of the bridge), they may never teach students at their present level (the left-hand side).

As in the case of the incremental versus comprehensive distinction, the difference is one of emphasis. Obviously, concerns for both children and subject matters—for both present and future—must be represented in "good" plans. Effective planning must simultaneously address both concerns.

Planning of Novice Versus Experienced Teachers. A final distinction in teacher planning stems from differences in the experience and expertise levels of teachers. Novice teachers view plans more as scripts than as guides; that is, these teachers are reluctant to vary from their plans. Part of the problem in this regard seems to be that they have not yet acquired the repertoire of skills and strategies that allow them to do so. A second part of this problem apparently stems from novices' lack of self-confidence, an obvious factor that can be traced to their lack of experience.

In contrast to novice teachers, experienced teachers view their plans primarily as guidelines; that is, the plans give direction and structure but are not scripts to be followed. As a consequence, experienced teachers do not hesitate to vary from their plans as the need arises (e.g., the teachable moment). Furthermore, they possess the skills and strategies they need to do so.

From an administrative point of view, then, although novice teachers may endorse and, in fact, welcome planning forms, experienced teachers may avoid and resent them, for at least two reasons. First, for experienced teachers, planning forms require far too much detail and resemble a contract more than a guide. Second, experienced teachers are more likely to plan in their heads, rather than to write down their plans (Morine-Dershimer & Vallance, 1976).

What Are the Key Components of Teacher Planning?

Effective teacher planning consists of four components: purpose, structure, assessment, and alternatives.

Purpose

Like teaching, teacher plans are purposeful. In the teacher's mind, planning is based on the following assumption: If the plans are implemented successfully, then certain goals or objectives will be accomplishments. These goals, objectives, or intended accomplishments define the purpose of the plan. In fact, the length of time addressed by the plan should correspond with the time needed by students to achieve its purpose.

To say that plans are purposeful does not imply that all purposes relate to students or, more specifically, to the three broad domains generally associated with purposes: cognitive, affective, and psychomotor (Oliva, 1993). There are "survival plans." The primary purpose of survival plans is to keep students busy and to make it through the lesson or day. There are "activity-oriented plans." The focus of such plans is on activities, rather than on outcomes, with either the hope that students will learn from the activities or the realization that different students may learn quite different things from the same activity. Although we acknowledge the presence of such plans, we suggest that most effective plans begin with some conceptualization of intended learning outcomes.

Structure

Structure includes three elements: activities, resources, and sequencing. Plans include the activities in which students are to engage to achieve the purpose. Are students to listen to lectures, participate in discussions, or complete prescribed work at their desks or tables? These are all examples of activities.

Plans also include the resources needed to participate in the activities. Do teachers need chalk and chalkboards, videocassette players, or computers (and, if so, how many)? Do students need books, access to libraries, or laboratory equipment? If so, are these resources available or likely to be available?

Finally, structure requires that careful attention be paid to sequencing. Not all things can be taught at the same time. Not all activities can be performed at the same time. By definition, certain things or activities must precede other things or activities. This order defines sequencing.

Several approaches to sequencing have been identified (Posner, 1994). Perhaps the most familiar approach is referred to as *task analysis* (Gagne & Briggs, 1974). Task analysis requires identifying the prerequisite knowledge and skills that are needed by students to achieve a particular goal. Once these prerequisites have been identified, they are sequenced accordingly. The major assumption underlying task analysis is that knowledge and skills exist in some type of hierarchy and that learning occurs as students move from lower positions on the hierarchy to upper ones. Thus, task analysis is based on a somewhat bottom-up approach to learning.

A somewhat competing approach to sequencing is based on the concept of advance organizers. *Advance organizers* are "appropriately relevant and inclusive introductory materials [which are] presented at a higher level of abstraction, generality, and inclusiveness than the content to be learned" (Ausubel, 1968, p. 148). If, for example, students are expected to learn a simple computer programming language, an advance organizer might present a model of the computer and include the relationship of each program statement to the model. In contrast to the task analysis approach, then, advance organizers represent a top-down approach to sequencing.

Other approaches to sequencing are inherent in the structure of the subject matter being taught. *Chronological sequencing* involves presenting material in some order that corresponds to the order in which events occurred. History lends itself to chronological sequencing, although we wonder whether reverse chronological sequencing may be more useful in helping students learn the antecedents and possible causes of various historical events.

Conceptual sequencing involves ordering based on relationships among the major concepts that define a subject matter. In mathematics, for example, natural (or counting) numbers typically are taught before whole numbers, which include the natural numbers plus zero. Whole numbers, in turn, usually precede integers (which include negative numbers). Conceptual sequencing is also appropriate in science (e.g., kingdoms, phyla, classes, orders) and social studies (e.g., neighborhoods, cities, states, countries).

Assessment

There must be some method to determine whether a plan is going according to schedule and whether the purpose of the plan is being achieved. Concerns pertaining to the implementation of the plan generally fall under the rubric "process evaluation" or "fidelity of implementation." Typically, observations or teacher logs are used to determine the degree to which the plan is implemented successfully.

Similarly, issues related to the achievement of the purpose of the plan typically have been addressed within the context of "product evaluation." In almost all cases, product evaluation requires data or evidence about or from students. How will teachers know whether students learned the difference between rhythm and tempo? Even when the purpose of a plan is to keep students busy, evidence must permit someone to determine how busy students were kept.

Alternatives

As everyone knows, there often is a vast difference between plans and reality. Successful teachers anticipate this possibility; that is, they consider the "worst case scenario." They ask questions like the following: What will I do if what I planned does not occur? What will I do if my plans do not lead to my intended goals? In response to these questions, these teachers design alternative activities within their plans. These alternatives provide teachers with the flexibility they need to ensure that plans become reality and that the outcomes of these plans are recognized.

Perhaps no other element of teaching differentiates novice from experienced teachers as much as the availability of alternative methods and procedures. Experienced teachers are far more likely to improvise on the spot, to make what are called "in-flight decisions." Furthermore, experienced teachers are far more likely to read situations and respond to them appropriately. Improvisation, "reading," and responding all require that alternatives be available to teachers.

Many of these alternatives can be planned. Within mastery learning (Bloom, 1968), such alternatives are referred to as "correctives" or "corrective instruction." Guskey (1985a) offered a useful set of alternatives that are available to all teachers, regardless of the propensity toward mastery learning.

Recommendations
Concerning Teacher Planning

On the basis of what is known about teacher planning, what recommendations can we offer teachers? Four fairly obvious recommendations follow.

Teachers should plan. Teacher planning is important for at least two reasons. First, vision has value. Vision permits contemplation of possibilities. Visionaries temporarily are freed from the constraints of reality. Because teaching effectiveness depends on both possibilities and constraints, unless teachers can visualize the future, they are unlikely to achieve their goals. Second, teacher planning transforms curriculum into instruction. This aspect of planning is particularly important when new curricula are being introduced. When this is the case, teachers report that they plan in order to "learn the subject matter themselves, to prepare or acquire needed curricular materials, and to make decisions about the content, pace, sequence, completeness and clarity of the curricular materials they have to work with" (Clark & Yinger, 1989, p. 229).

As mentioned earlier, the downside of planning is fairly obvious. Planning requires time, a commodity that teachers typically lack. Many teachers are simply too busy to plan; others, although having planning time, use it for more immediate activities other than planning. Simply stated, planning and teaching both require substantial amounts of time. If teachers are paid only to teach, they will spend most of their time teaching. Planning either will go by the wayside or will occur during out-of-school time.

Teachers should make a real effort to plan immediately before school starts and during the first few weeks of school. Evidence suggests that planning during the first weeks of school has long-term effects (Clark & Yinger, 1989). This early planning establishes a framework of rules, routines, schedules, expectations, and groupings of students that has long-term effects for the remainder of the school year. Minor adjustments are made in this framework up through early October; by mid-October, the framework in place remains in place for the remainder of the school year.

Teachers need to envision plans as guides, not as scripts. Classroom life is simply too complex to negotiate with predetermined ways of behaving. Most teachers have experienced a wonderfully planned classroom activity that turned out to be a "bomb." Needed materials and equipment are not always available. Interruptions occur for any number of reasons. On the one hand, the scripted teacher is likely to have difficulty dealing with this complexity. The flexible teacher, on the other hand, is able to adapt to the demands of the situation.

Teachers must know when and how to vary from their plans. Adapting randomly is no virtue. Rather, good teachers are able to "read" their students. They know which students are doing well and which are having difficulty. They know the areas in which students are having problems. They know what their students know and have yet to learn. They know the misunderstandings their students have developed.

The ability to read students is part artistic and part scientific. Some teachers appear to be more intuitive than others; that is, they sense what their students know and do not know and which students know what. Nonetheless, virtually all teachers benefit from a bit of data. Examining students' performances on daily assignments, quizzes, and standardized tests provides teachers with a potential wealth of information.

The ability to read students provides teachers with the "when" of adaptation. The availability of alternative strategies, activities, and resources influences the "how" of adaptation. Teachers who enter the classroom with a single strategy or activity and limited resources are unable to adapt. Teachers must plan for adaptation.

Teacher Leaders and Teacher Planning

Teacher leaders have several roles to play in enhancing teacher planning. Four of these roles are addressed in this section: (a) providing peer review of teacher plans, (b) "buying" planning time for teachers, (c) engaging in discussion of the need for multilevel planning, and (d) emphasizing and arranging opportunities for collaborative planning.

Peer Review of Teacher Plans

Once plans are prepared, some type of review is important if the plans, in U.S. Army terminology, are to "be all that they can be." Two issues should be addressed before teachers' plans are reviewed: (a) Who should review the plans? and (b) On what basis should the plans be reviewed? In our opinion, these are related, not separate, issues.

TABLE 4.1 Criteria for Reviewing Teacher Plans

---

1. Is the purpose/goal of the lesson/unit made clear?

2. Are the activities likely to engage students in the process of learning (are they likely to be excited about the activities or bored to tears)?

3. Are the activities likely to lead students to the attainment of the lesson/unit purpose/goal?

4. Are the needed materials and other instructional resources (e.g., computer software, videotapes) available and accessible?

5. Is the time to be devoted to the lesson/unit specified? If so, does it seem reasonable?

6. Does the plan specify a way to gauge and/or monitor purpose/goal attainment?

7. Does the plan include provisions to provide students initially not attaining the purpose/goal opportunities to do so? If so, do these provisions seem reasonable?

Self-review is useful, particularly if teachers have the luxury of being able to put the plans aside for a period of time. Self-review permits teachers to reexamine the plans in the "cold light of day." Do the plans still seem appropriate and reasonable? Will the activities maintain student involvement and ultimately lead to the attainment of the desired ends? Will the needed resources be available? These are the types of questions that can be addressed through self-review.

Peer review is extremely useful. Plans generally are improved if they are reviewed from equally knowledgeable persons operating from slightly different points of view. For peer review to be effective, however, it must be conducted within an atmosphere of trust. Peers must truly be peers (not just "other teachers"). Furthermore, the evaluative nature of peer review must be downplayed, and the supportive and facilitative aspects must be emphasized. Table 4.1 includes a set of criteria that can be used either by teachers themselves or by peers to review plans.

Administrative review is generally the least useful type of review. At least three reasons can be given in support of this contention. First, despite recent calls for instructional leadership on the part of school administrators (Greenfield, 1987), the realities are that many principals do not have the time necessary for direct instructional leadership (Anderson & Shirley, in press). By "direct," we mean that the principal is involved in discussion of instructional issues, takes part in instructional staff development activities, and engages in clinical or development supervision of instruction. Many principals who are viewed as instructional leaders by their teaching staff tend to be involved in indirect leadership; that is, they communicate to teachers the importance of good instruction, and they support teachers in their instructional efforts (e.g., by providing needed resources).

Second, principals often lack the depth of knowledge needed to provide constructive criticism of the plans they review. For example, secondary school principals with a background in music quite likely will have little of substance to say about the plans of a science teacher. Moreover, many principals may have completed only a single course in instruction or instructional supervision. In contrast, an increasing number of teachers have master's degrees in teaching.

Third, principals generally conduct their reviews under severe time constraints and for multiple reasons. Principals are required to review the plans of all teachers in their schools (whether there are 20, 50, 100, or more). Furthermore, although a principal may inform his or her faculty that the primary purpose of the review is to help teachers improve their planning, almost always the overriding concern is for whether teachers are "doing their jobs." Thus, principals typically find themselves simultaneously engaged in *formative* and *summative* evaluation (Scriven, 1967).

Both self- and peer review can focus on the psychological and ecological aspects of planning; that is, these reviews can address such questions as "What is the likely impact of these plans on students?"—a psychological question—and "How can I ensure that the plans are implemented properly?"—an ecological one. In contrast, for all of the reasons mentioned above, administrative reviews are almost always conducted within a technological context.

Buying Planning Time

It is quite clear that the culture of teaching undervalues planning. As mentioned earlier, planning typically comes out of the hides of teachers. Teacher leaders must work toward changing that culture. Two foci of these changes are possible: (a) time within the school year and (b) extensions of the school year.

Within the school year, teacher leaders can work toward ensuring that all teachers have daily planning periods. This change is particularly important for elementary school teachers because many secondary school teachers already have a planning period. All teachers will likely benefit from the availability of one planning period each day.

Once planning periods are made available, they must be scheduled. In this regard, common planning periods are essential. The "commonness" of these planning periods may reflect similarities across teachers in terms of the subjects taught (typically at the secondary school level) or the age or grade levels of students taught (typically at the elementary school level). This commonness also may reflect differences in the level of students being taught by the teachers (e.g., remedial, "regular," gifted or advanced). Common planning periods reduce the idiosyncrasies of teachers, reflect concern for the whole or total child, and recognize the need for integrating curricula.

Most of the planning that occurs within the school year is oriented toward daily or lesson planning. Planning that addresses unit and course concerns typically requires the availability of time outside the traditional school year (e.g., summers, weekends). Quite clearly, extra time requires extra compensation. Thus, teacher leaders must work toward securing external funding to support such planning activities. The first step in securing such funding is the preparation of a proposal. Proposals for external funding must meet at least five criteria: (a) a clear, defensible purpose (e.g., the development of integrated curricula in the upper elementary grades); (b) an explicit set of activities and tasks that can be expected to lead to the accomplishment of the purpose of the proposal; (c) a plan for determining and evaluating this accomplishment; (d) the human and material resources needed to carry out the proposed work; and (e) an adequate and reasonable budget for carrying out the work. In addition to being familiar with these criteria, teacher leaders must become familiar with various sources of funding (both government and private).

Multilevel Planning

Teacher leaders must help teachers realize the layered nature of planning. Earlier, we spoke of two types of planners—incremental and comprehensive. In our opinion, hybrid planners are likely to be the most effective. Comprehensive planning (e.g., course, unit) provides the overall framework to ensure the plans are likely to be *effective* in achieving their purposes or goals. Similarly, incremental planning (e.g., lesson, daily) is essential if the comprehensive plans are to be *workable.*

Planning is likely to be most effective if it begins with the big picture and moves to the details. Thus, comprehensive planning should precede incremental planning. On the one hand, comprehensive plans are like the picture on the cover of a jigsaw puzzle box. They give teachers the general guidelines they need to make judgments on the adequacy of what they are doing. Incremental plans, on the other hand, are similar to the strategies used to put the puzzle together. Puzzle doers may sort the pieces by shape or color, or they may begin by forming the border of the puzzle. All of these steps are elements of incremental planning.

Seminars and discussion groups may be the best vehicle for teacher leaders to help teachers develop these insights. Transparencies such as the one shown in Figure 4.2 may be useful as starting points for such discussions.

The transparency shown in Figure 4.2 can be used to address a number of key issues. First, from a curriculum perspective, what are the differences among aims, goals, and objectives? (Answer: They closely correspond to courses, units, and lessons.) Second, also from a curriculum point of view, how can lessons and units be organized and sequenced to increase the likelihood that the course aims can be achieved? Third, what can teachers do to

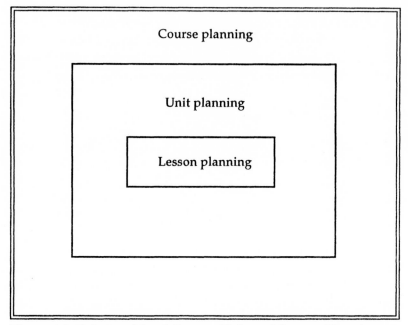

Figure 4.2. Relationship of Course, Unit, and Lesson Planning

ensure that they do not lose "the forest for the trees"? All of these questions are worthy of careful discussion and deliberation.

Collaborative Planning

Partly because of the nature of teacher planning, planning is often done is isolation. We addressed this issue briefly in our discussion of the need for common planning periods. However, the simple existence of common planning periods does not ensure that collaborative planning takes place. We can envision a situation in which a common planning time is available and teachers work in isolation on their plans. If common planning periods are to be effective, then collaborative planning is necessary.

Collaborative planning requires that teachers work together to develop their plans. Thus, collaborative planning is particularly important at the course level, although it may be beneficial at smaller levels of planning. At the course level, collaborative planning is necessary for two reasons.

First, it ensures that the content and objectives of a course represent the collective wisdom of the faculty, not the idiosyncratic views of a teacher. Almost every teacher has had the experience of taking a course whose content depended more on the whims of the teacher than on the structure of the subject matter. This assertion is not to imply that teachers should adhere rigidly to course outlines established by book companies, district officials, or their fellow teachers. Rather, it is to suggest that unbridled license to teach what one wants is not a characteristic of the teaching profession.

Second, collaborative planning increases the probability that courses will be designed within the context of other courses at the same age/grade level or similar courses at different age/grade levels. Designing courses that are related to one another at a particular age or grade level is referred to as *horizontal curriculum integration*. Similarly, designing courses that provide appropriate learning experiences for students over time is termed *vertical curriculum integration*. In recent years, there has been a great deal of talk about curriculum integration. In contrast, there has been relatively little action. A likely cause of this inaction is one of the central themes of this chapter—namely, the lack of time for teacher planning.

Closing Comment

The importance of planning was emphasized throughout this chapter. Little else needs to be added in this regard. However, one aspect of planning needs to be emphasized in closing. Plans have a greater chance of being implemented successfully if they are communicated to the students. As Clark and Yinger (1989) pointed out:

Planning itself is given inadequate attention in preservice and inservice teacher preparation, but usually is addressed at some level; communication of plans to students is almost never addressed. Yet success or failure of this link

between thought and action can make a substantial difference between whether a plan is merely a grandiose
entry in a plan book, or becomes the description of a lesson
or activity well executed. (p. 230)

Just as planning is especially important during the initial
weeks of a school year, communication of plans to students is
particularly important during this time and during times of transition between activities and subject matters. It should be emphasized that communication of plans to students need not be
simply oral. The way materials are organized by the teacher,
whether the teacher begins a lesson on time, how the teacher reacts
when plans go awry—all of these communicate to students about
the nature and importance of plans and planning.

Communicating plans to students has obvious benefits for the
students themselves. It is important to note, however, that such
communication is also beneficial to teachers. As Clark and Yinger
(1989) wrote: "The more imaginative the thought invested in communication of teacher plans to students, the more likely those
plans are to come to fruition without undue confusion, delay, or
back-tracking" (p. 230). And, isn't this the goal of all teachers?

5

Helping Teachers
Teach Effectively

Unlike some school administrators, teacher leaders are likely to have immediate credibility with classroom teachers. When it comes to instructional matters, most teacher leaders are perceived as educators who can *demonstrate*, not just talk about, teaching practices and strategies. For many experienced teachers, these practices and strategies have become automatic. Faced with a group of students, they just know what to do. As a consequence, many experienced teachers may not have analyzed their teaching practices and strategies to determine what makes them effective. To improve the teaching of other teachers, teacher leaders must be able to identify the critical components of effective teaching practices and to share with their teacher colleagues strategies for improvement.

The purpose of this chapter is to provide teacher leaders a summary of research on effective teaching practices and a description of strategies they can use to help their teaching colleagues become better teachers. More specifically, this chapter addresses the following questions:

- What is an effective teacher?
- How can teachers create classroom environments that are physically appealing and psychologically comfortable for students?
- How can teachers improve their communication with students?
- What are the most effective teaching practices?

What Is an Effective Teacher?

Simply stated, an effective teacher is one who is able to bring about intended learning in his or her students. This definition implies that the teacher is able to identify what he or she intends students to learn, structure learning experiences to facilitate student learning, and determine whether or to what extent the intended learning has occurred.

There is no question that some teachers are more effective than others. But what accounts for these differences in effectiveness? This question has sparked considerable debate in the past and will undoubtedly continue to do so. Although some people argue that teaching is an art and therefore can be neither objectified nor duplicated, others contend there is a scientific basis for effective teaching. Arguing for the "teaching-as-art" view, Thomas (1975) explained:

> One becomes a good teacher in the same way one becomes a good actor, a good poet, a good musician, a good painter. One develops a unique style, a personalized method, a way of teaching that cannot be mass produced or even replicated. . . . Some teachers are great; some, average; some, poor. No one has yet been able to identify what makes one person a better teacher than another. We can recognize the art, but we cannot identify its separate common components. . . . A good teacher is one that teaches well, much as a good surgeon operates with skill. What makes a good teacher or a good poet or a good surgeon

only the stars know; and they are not, as yet, willing to tell us the secret. (p. 61)

Although acknowledging that teaching contains elements of artistry, Gage (1978), Hunter (1976), Rosenshine (1986), and others assert that much of what is recognized as effective teaching is of a scientific or technical nature. Arguing from this perspective, it stands to reason, then, that effective teaching practices can be both identified and replicated. Based on our combined 50-plus years of experience teaching and analyzing teaching, we are convinced that effective teaching is a combination of both art and science. Although teaching does involve certain difficult-to-describe intangibles, it also involves specific practices that can be taught. The challenge for teacher leaders is first to identify effective teaching practices and then to help more teachers use them more frequently in the classroom.

What do effective teachers do? They address the needs of their students in terms of both what they teach and how they teach. Effective teachers recognize that although teaching is generally a group activity, learning is a very individual one. Although the 25 students seated in Ms. Harrison's math class may all see the same teacher and hear the same words, their experiences will differ. The skilled teacher is sensitive to these differences and takes actions to address them so that, ideally, each student is provided an optimal learning experience.

A key factor affecting learning is the student's level of involvement or engagement in the process of learning. Extensive research indicates that the higher the level of student involvement, the more likely it is that learning will occur. Although each student ultimately determines the degree to which he or she will be involved in learning, the teacher's attitude and behavior can either enhance or impede the student's involvement. Factors such as the classroom's physical environment, the student's level of psychological comfort in the classroom, and the quality of communication between teacher and student affect involvement. To a large extent, the teacher can significantly influence each of these critical factors.

Creating a Desirable
Physical Environment in the Classroom

If asked to visualize a classroom, most people would focus first on its physical qualities. They might see four walls, student desks, and a chalkboard. They might notice the aesthetic aspects of the classroom: Are the colors pleasing? Is the room attractive and tidy or drab and cluttered? Is student work displayed?

They might focus also on other aspects of the physical environment: Is the classroom temperature comfortable? Is the lighting appropriate? Are the student desks comfortable? Is there noise interference (e.g., is the classroom next to a band room or playground)?

Although individual teachers are unlikely to be involved in many decisions regarding the physical environment (e.g., choice of student desks, location of classroom, type of lighting), they do decide how the physical environment will be organized. For example, although they may not select the types of student desks in their classrooms, teachers typically decide how the desks will be arranged. This might appear to be a relatively innocuous decision; it is not. The arrangement of student desks can facilitate or inhibit student interaction, as well as affect student behavior and attitudes. Stated simply, the greater the extent to which the physical environment supports the teaching practices that occur within it, the more likely it is that the intended learning will occur (Barker, 1964).

To illustrate the importance of the physical arrangement of the classroom to instruction, assume that Teacher A plans to facilitate a discussion with her class, whereas Teacher B plans to use the chalkboard as he lectures. How would the seating arrangement in the two classrooms differ? To accomplish her objective, Teacher A, on the one hand, would need an arrangement that facilitates both student-to-student and teacher-to-student interaction (e.g., desks arranged in a circle). Teacher B, on the other hand, wants students to watch what he writes and to listen to what he says. In this case, students might be seated in straight rows facing the teacher and the chalkboard (but not facing each other). To be maximally effective, then, a teacher must view seating arrangements as dynamic, not as fixed, permanent conditions.

Once the teacher has decided how the desks will be arranged, it is equally important to decide who will sit where. This decision should be based on the teacher's knowledge of research, as well as his or her knowledge of the students. The results of several studies suggest that where students sit can affect significantly the quality of their relationship with the teacher and their level of involvement in the learning process.

In a 3-year longitudinal study, for example, Rist (1970) found that students assigned to seats farthest from their teachers had the fewest interactions with them, were the least involved in classroom activities, and had the lowest achievement scores. Conversely, students assigned to seats closest to their teachers had the highest levels of involvement, received the most teacher time, and had the highest achievement scores. The closer students are to the teacher, the more likely they will be involved.

The implications of such findings are obvious: Teachers need to find ways to be physically close to their students, especially students who experience problems with learning. Although it is impossible for every child to be seated next to the teacher all the time, the teacher who manages the classroom by walking around can be next to every child at different times during the class period. In this regard, several researchers report that the more frequently teachers sit at their desks, the lower their students' achievement. Given such findings, McGreal (1983) concluded, "A good pair of comfortable shoes is a necessary teaching tool" (p. 82).

In addition to affecting student involvement in learning, decisions about how seats are arranged and who sits where can have significant implications for students' attitudes and their classroom behavior. Often, elementary school seating arrangements reflect the teacher's desire to separate students into subgroups. The basis for the separation is important. The seating arrangement may be designed to separate students into subgroups based on their ability. Despite the fact that the negative effects of ability grouping outweigh the positive effects, some type of ability grouping continues to be practiced in almost four fifths of America's classrooms (Oakes, 1985).

An alternative to ability grouping is cooperative learning (Johnson & Johnson, 1989). In a nutshell, *cooperative learning* is a form of grouping within a class that promotes interaction among students of differing ability and achievement levels. With this approach, students are assigned to heterogenous learning groups in which they work together to complete assignments. Studies of cooperative learning have found consistently that this approach results in increased student achievement, more positive race relations, and increased self-esteem (Slavin, 1994). Despite these findings, however, grouping patterns that promote cooperative learning rarely are observed in classrooms.

Whatever the physical arrangement of the classroom, teacher leaders need to remind teachers that their decisions about the arrangement of desks and the assignment of students to them are not insignificant. A teacher's judgments about seating arrangements, in fact, can have long-term social, psychological, and educational implications for students.

Creating Psychologically Comfortable Classroom Environments

"Think about the best teacher you ever had and, in one sentence, identify the quality that made him or her special." Each semester we ask our students to engage in this exercise. Almost without exception, the qualities our students identify most often have to do with the teacher's ability to relate to them as individuals. Comments such as, "She made me feel special," "He cared about me," and "She kept telling me I could succeed" are typical responses.

In addition to teaching them knowledge and skills, teachers also help students define who they are. From daily interactions with teachers, students learn whether they are important or insignificant, bright or slow, liked or despised. Teachers transmit these messages by their facial expressions and gestures, the way they speak to students, the amount of time they devote to individual students, the number of times they choose to approach a student, and numerous other ways. From the messages that they receive, students decide whether they are willing to risk participation in class activities. Those who receive messages of acceptance and inclusion are more likely to risk participation and interaction; those who do not are less likely. Effective teachers recognize that student involvement does not come easy; it requires a trusting, psychologically comfortable classroom environment.

What is such an environment? It is a classroom where students are affirmed and respected, where all students feel free to participate, where the unique talents and skills of each student are celebrated and developed, and where the dignity of students with special needs is preserved. Sizer (1984) summed it up in the seventh of his nine principles of "essential schools": "The tone of the school should explicitly and self-consciously stress values of unanxious expectations ('I won't threaten you, but I expect much of you'), of trust, and of decency" (Sizer, 1984, p. 187).

As the population of America's classrooms changes, the need for creating psychologically comfortable classroom environments will increase. In fact, one of the most formidable challenges facing tomorrow's schools will be how to build students' self-esteem. By the year 2000, one third of the children in America's classrooms will come from economically disadvantaged homes (Reed & Sautter, 1990). Many of these "at-risk" children will enter school with both physical and psychological deficiencies. Whether they remain at risk will depend, to a large extent, on what happens to them in classrooms. If America's classroom environments are threatening and hostile to one third of its children, not only will the future of these children be at risk but so will its future as a country.

It is important to note that although we acknowledge an undeniable relationship between a child's socioeconomic status and his or her propensity to be at risk, we are convinced that socioeconomic status does not necessarily determine how much a student may or may not be at risk. We maintain, instead, that the critical factors in determining whether a child is at risk are (a) the child's level of dependency on the school and (b) the degree to which the school addresses that dependency. In other words, the school plays a significant role in determining whether a child remains at risk.

Because children from economically disadvantaged back-grounds often have limited resources, their level of dependency on the school for the resources they lack is typically high. Our definition of *resources* includes not only educational materials (e.g., books, computers) but also human resources (e.g., people who value education and transmit that value to students). On the one hand, when it comes to education, schools often provide the "sole source" for too many economically disadvantaged children. Children from middle- and upper-income families, on the other hand, are likely to have support structures outside the school. Thus they are less dependent on the school for their education.

To illustrate the role of the school for students from advan-taged and disadvantaged backgrounds, consider the following scenario. Imagine you are observing a geometry class in which the teacher, Ms. Jones, does a poor job explaining the content. Fearing embarrassment and ridicule, neither James nor Johnny asks for further clarification despite the fact that both are thoroughly con-fused. As they leave the classroom, Johnny expresses concern, but James does not. James, a middle-class student, says to Johnny, a lower-class student, "I'll get my mom to explain this stuff to me tonight." Johnny nods his head but can only hope that he will be able to solve the problem himself. Because James has resources available to him outside the school, his level of dependency on Ms. Jones is considerably lower than Jimmy's. His chances of learning geometry *in spite of* Ms. Jones's poor instruction are quite good. He does not have to risk embarrassment by asking questions in class. Johnny's chances of learning geometry, however, are not very promising. Whether or not he learns it will depend a great deal on what happens in the classroom. If instruction continues to be poor and the classroom environment continues to be so threat-ening that he is afraid to seek clarification, Johnny is likely not only to fail geometry but also to develop negative attitudes about himself and his ability to succeed in school. Such an environment makes Johnny at risk both academically and psychologically.

What are some of the characteristics of psychologically com-fortable classrooms? Such environments are characterized by clearly communicated expectations, a sense of fairness, and mu-tual respect. Let's consider each of these in some detail.

Clearly Communicated Expectations

An effective teacher realizes that if students are to feel psychologically comfortable, they must know what is expected of them; security comes partly from knowing the rules of the game. Thus, teachers should establish rules and spend considerable time communicating and explaining them to students.

Although necessary for an orderly, secure environment, rules should be realistic, reasonable, well defined, limited in number, and clearly understood. They should be stated in such a way that it is obvious whether a specific behavior violates a rule. Instead of saying, "Students should be prepared for class," the teacher might say, "Students should bring their books to class." Only the second example specifies the desired behavior. In addition, rules should be stated positively. Instead of saying, "Do not throw paper on the floor," a teacher might say, "Please use the trash can as needed."

Who should determine the rules in classrooms? Some teachers would argue that students should be involved in the process of establishing rules; others, that it is the teacher's prerogative and responsibility to define acceptable behavior. We suggest a compromise. The teacher might select a limited number of nonnegotiable rules and then allow students to add others. In addition, the establishment of rules depends a great deal on the age and developmental level of students. For primary school students, on the one hand, the rules established by teachers are part of the socialization process. For secondary school students, on the other hand, permitting their input into the governance of the classroom recognizes their pending adulthood.

Enforcement of rules should be done fairly and promptly but not harshly. When dealing with student misbehavior, teachers should be careful to "separate the sin from the sinner." A teacher's response should indicate clearly that he or she is rejecting the student's behavior—not the student. For example, instead of saying, "Andy, you are a very bad boy," the teacher might say, "Andy, I do not like the fact that you took Jane's paper without her permission. Please return it to her now so that we can continue our lesson." When responding to student misbehavior, teachers should remain calm as they make their point quickly and firmly. Once the point has been made, the teacher should continue with the lesson with as little loss of time as possible.

Y. Ginott (1972) (just kidding; it's really H. Ginott, but "why gnot" is much funnier) suggests three steps that teachers might follow in addressing student misbehavior: (a) Describe what they see, (b) describe what they feel, and (c) describe what needs to be done. Such an approach keeps the focus on the behavior, rather than on the person.

Students need structure in their lives. Rules provide that structure. Classrooms that lack rules, classrooms in which rules go unenforced, or classroom in which rules are enforced inconsistently fail to provide students the order and predictability so critical to their development.

A Sense of Fairness

Fairness is a quality associated with psychologically comfortable classrooms. But what does it mean to be fair? Does fair mean treating all students the same? No. Fairness means treating an individual in an impartial manner, basing this treatment on the needs of the student and the conditions in place at a given point in time. At the same time, however, the "welfare of the group" must be considered.

The notion that "fair does not mean equal treatment" is often difficult for students (and even some parents) to understand. To facilitate their understanding, teachers might have students respond to a situation such as the following:

> You have two grown children. The older is a highly successful businessman who has been able to provide his family with the very best that money can buy. His 18-year-old son is graduating from high school, and your son wants to buy him a new BMW. Your son has had some bad luck in the stock market lately and asks you to lend him $8,000 to make a down payment on his son's car. At the same time, your daughter, a single parent with three children, calls. Since her divorce 6 years ago, she has struggled to provide her three children with a modest lifestyle. Much to her

dismay, she has learned that her youngest child needs an operation for a heart condition that could be fatal. She has no medical insurance and asks you to lend her $8,000 to cover her son's hospitalization costs. You have only $8,000 to lend. What do you do?

Few students are likely to argue that the mother should divide the money equally between her children (the traditional "fair" response). Because the needs of the children are so different, the mother's response to their requests would differ. Teachers who seek to be fair by allocating resources equally to students without regard for their individual needs are, in fact, acting unfairly.

In classrooms characterized by a sense of fairness, the teacher ensures that all students have access to learning opportunities. Being fair may mean spending more time with those students who truly need the time, rather than with those who demand it. Several researchers have found that in classrooms ranging from preschool through graduate school, some students are given considerably more opportunities to participate than others. Sadker and Sadker (1986), for example, after studying more than 100 fourth-, sixth-, and eighth-grade classrooms in four states and the District of Columbia, identified two groups of students: "the haves and the have nots of teacher attention" (p. 513). The "haves" were the male students; the "have nots" were the female students. The researchers concluded that male students received more attention from teachers, were given more time to talk in classrooms, were involved in more interaction, and received more feedback than female students. This was true whether they needed it or not.

Good (1981) also studied teacher-student interactions in classrooms and found that teachers behaved differently toward students on the basis of the teacher's perception of the student's ability. Students classified as low achieving (typically those from lower socioeconomic status) had significantly fewer opportunities for participation in class activities. They were seated farther away from the teacher, received less attention, were called on less frequently, were interrupted more, were given less wait time to respond to the teacher's questions, received less feedback on their progress, and were provided less demanding work.

Suffice it to say that if students do not feel a sense of fairness in how the teacher runs the classroom and interacts with students, it is unlikely that they will be willing to get into the game. Instead, most would prefer simply to observe the action from the sidelines.

Mutual Respect

A quality essential to a psychologically comfortable classroom environment is mutual respect. Too often, discussions of this quality focus on the necessity of students respecting teachers, rather than vice versa. Our experience has led us to conclude that respect is a two-way street. Furthermore, respect cannot be mandated or demanded; it must be earned.

In psychologically comfortable classrooms, each student is made to feel like "somebody," a person of worth. One of the major fears of students (as well as everyone else) is the threat of invisibility—the fear that no one will notice them. During an interview with several students enrolled at a highly successful alternative school for students who had either dropped out or been pushed out of their regular high schools, they all commented on their feelings of invisibility at their former schools:

> I just couldn't function with a whole bunch of kids. The teacher didn't even know I was there until I caused trouble.

> I would just sit in the back of the class and hide behind the girl in front of me. And the teacher didn't even know I was there. Sometimes I'd go to sleep. Nobody paid me any attention.

> The teacher gave too much work in one period. She acted like everybody was smart. I tried my best, but I got tired of failing, but she just didn't seem to care.

After repeated negative messages that tell students they are not valued or respected, many students actually seek the very status they fear most—invisibility. They sit as far away from the teacher as possible and, if given a choice, do not participate in class activities. Or, they may engage in negative behaviors simply to gain attention. Unfortunately, these students may not realize that such behaviors ultimately may result in suspension or expulsion, actions that literally make students invisible in the school environment. Finally, in many of the major urban cities in America, more than half of America's high school students are choosing to make themselves permanently invisible: They drop out (Kunisawa, 1988).

How do teachers demonstrate respect for their students? First, they acknowledge their students as individuals. Teachers learn students' names quickly so that interactions with them can be personal. When a student returns to school after being absent, the teacher lets the student know that he or she was missed.

Second, teachers who respect students also listen to them. As they listen, they maintain eye contact and, if appropriate, repeat the student's message to show that they heard and understood what the student was saying. Skilled teachers are both active and empathic listeners. They listen to hear not only what students are saying but also what they might not be saying.

Finally, teachers who respect students display confidence and trust in the students' ability and potential. These teachers communicate high expectations for their students and then coach them throughout the learning process so that they can reach those expectations.

Despite a teacher's efforts, at many times the students may make it especially difficult for the teacher to model respect. These are the times that count most. After all, the teacher is the adult. The issue here is whether the teacher can look beyond the student's immediate misbehavior and see a person worthy of respect. Teachers who pass this test gain credibility not only as teachers but also, and more important, as genuinely caring human beings.

As Sizer (1984) pointed out, mutual respect transcends the classroom door. Thus, teacher leaders have the responsibility of creating an atmosphere of respect at the school level. The psychological environment of each classroom must be modeled after and reinforced by the psychological environment of the school. Such modeling and reinforcement are keys to creating the kind of workplace in which teachers are happy to ply their trade.

Effective Classroom Communication

As teachers, you undoubtedly have taught and may have had the opportunity to observe many lessons. Stop reading for a moment and think about the best lesson you either taught or observed and try to recall the unique techniques and features that made it effective.

Some of you might have recalled that the teacher used clear, vivid examples; others might have remembered that the teacher organized the presentation so that it was easy to follow; still others might have remembered that the teacher reinforced students' responses and provided feedback. All of these techniques are important to effective teaching.

Just as effective teachers use rules to structure their classroom environments, they also follow guidelines to structure their presentations. Relying on age-old folk wisdom, Hunter (1976) wrote that most good communication involves three simple steps: (a) Tell students what you are going to tell them, (b) tell them, and (c) tell them what you told them. In other words, teachers should (a) introduce the lesson, (b) explain the lesson, and (c) summarize the lesson.

Introducing the Lesson

Effective teachers get students involved at the very outset by using a variety of techniques. One method for introducing the lesson is simply to *state the objective:* to state the purpose of the lesson and let students know what is expected of them. For example, the teacher might say, "Today we will be studying the respiratory system. By the end of the class period, I want you to identify each of the parts of the respiratory system and describe its function." By stating the objective, the teacher communicates his or her expectation that students will be active learners.

A second method for introducing the lesson is to begin with a *review.* The teacher might ask questions about what was learned during the previous lesson, have students check each other's homework, or ask students for feedback on homework items with which they had difficulty. By reviewing the previous lesson, the teacher is able to reinforce previous learning, as well as to determine whether students are ready to begin a new lesson. Furthermore, review permits the teacher to make connections between what is to be learned and what students already know or can do.

A third method for introducing a lesson is to create what Hunter (1976) referred to as an *"instructional set,"* or perhaps more appropriately, a motivational framework for learning. Such a framework piques students' interests and prepares them for the lesson. For example, when beginning the lesson on the respiratory system, the teacher might say, "Suppose you see a man lying on the sidewalk. He is not moving, and his eyes are closed. What might you do to determine whether he is alive?" By beginning the lesson in this way, the teacher hopes to capture students' attention and whet their appetites for a discussion of the respiratory system.

Although no single method is best for introducing a lesson, an effective teacher recognizes the need for orienting students to what they are working toward, motivating students to put forth effort needed to learn, and helping students form associations between what they have learned and what they are expected to learn. Thus, combinations of the aforementioned methods, as well as unique methods developed by teacher, can be used.

Explaining the Lesson

Once the teacher has introduced the lesson, a second phase begins: explaining the lesson. Given the fact that, in most classrooms, teachers talk about two thirds of the time (Flanders, 1965), the need to ensure the quality of teacher talk is evident. Studies suggest that teachers can improve the quality of their communication by using certain strategies.

Structure the Lesson. Teachers should structure the lesson very carefully. During the planning process, they should decide the basic content to be taught and then organize it so that it can be presented in its simplest, clearest form. Suppose, for example, the objective of the lesson is "Students will write a five-sentence paragraph." In structuring the content, a teacher may begin with a discussion of the meaning of "topic sentence." To simplify the concept, the teacher might give students a list of words or short phrases and ask them to identify the word or phrase in the list that is broad enough to cover the others in the list.

After students have demonstrated the ability to identify main ideas from a list of words or phrases, the teacher might then give them a list of words or phrases and ask them to generate a word or phrase that could encompass all the items on the list and thus serve as the main idea. Once the students have demonstrated the ability to complete these tasks, the teacher could move on to activities related to developing supporting sentences and concluding statements (if appropriate and necessary).

The point of this illustration is not to suggest that this approach for teaching students to write a paragraph should be used as a model. Instead, teachers should determine the ultimate purpose of the lesson (in terms of student learning) and then develop and organize activities and explanations in a series of steps that will help students achieve that desired result.

Use Examples and Analogies. The most effective way to make learning come alive is through the use of examples and/or analogies. Effective teachers provide their students with specific, clear, and meaningful examples and carefully thought-out analogies to illustrate the new learning and to link this learning with what the students already know or have experienced. Most examples and analogies should be planned before, not during, the presentation. At the same time, however, teachers should know their subject well enough to be able to create examples and analogies on the spot.

Use Verbal Cues. No matter how attentive a student might try to be, there will be moments of disengagement. Through the use of verbal cues, the teacher signals the student that important information is about to be presented. Examples of verbal cues are statements such as, "Now listen very carefully," "Pay attention now. The next point is very important," and "Does everyone have his or her ears turned on?" Such signals serve to reengage students who might be momentarily disengaged.

Address Multiple Learning Modalities. Teachers can increase student involvement by addressing multiple learning modalities during the lesson presentation. The term *learning modality* refers to the different ways people receive and process information. Some people receive and process information primarily through the *auditory* modality; they need to hear the material, and they learn. Others receive and process information primarily through the *visual* modality; they need to see the concept illustrated or written down, and they learn. Still others are primarily *kinesthetic* or *tactile* learners; they need to manipulate or feel the material, and they learn.

To increase the likelihood that all students will be involved, teachers should appeal to multiple modalities when teaching. When discussing a new vocabulary word, for example, the teacher might *say* the word (for the auditory learner) and then *write* it on the board (for the visual learner). Or, the teacher who is teaching the parts of the circulatory system might use a life-size model of the human body. Students could *hear* about the parts of the system, *see* them, and *trace* them.

Check for Understanding. Once the lesson has been introduced and appropriate explanations have been given, the teacher has two options. The first is simply to *assume that all students understood what they were being taught.* The second option is to *check out the validity of that assumption.* Effective teachers tend to do the latter. They create opportunities for their students to express what they do and do not understand. Perhaps the most common method of doing this is to ask questions. Indeed, John Dewey (1933) regarded questions as "the very core of teaching" (p. 266).

During a typical school day, a typical teacher asks between 300 and 400 questions. Although teachers obviously recognize questioning as a powerful teaching strategy, only about 20% of the questions they ask require critical thought (e.g., questions that usually begin with *why, how,* or *what if*). The overwhelming majority (about 60%) of teachers' questions require students to recall information (e.g., questions that usually begin with *who, what,* or *when*) (Gall, 1970).

Contrary to popular opinion, questions that require thinking are not "better" than those that require memory. The key issue is whether the types of questions asked are consistent with the objectives of the lesson. On the one hand, if the lesson's objective is "Students will name the parts of the respiratory system," questions that require student recall of information are most appropriate. On the other hand, if the objective of the lesson is "Students will analyze the role of the American troops in Operation Desert Storm," so-called higher-order questions are necessary.

Given the importance of questions, a number of studies have focused on what happens in the classroom after teachers pose questions. Research findings reveal that although teachers ask lots of questions, they do not provide students a great deal of time to answer them. In fact, researchers have coined the phrase "wait time" to denote the period of silence between the time the teacher asks a question and the time the student responds (Rowe, 1972). In many classrooms, only 1 or 2 seconds of silence is given. Teachers who allow students such a limited time to respond fail to consider that students differ in the time needed to process information and that higher order questions require more time for students to process than do simple recall questions.

When wait time is increased to 3 to 5 seconds, students tend to provide longer answers and to give more responses and are more likely to give correct responses. Furthermore, students tend to show more confidence in their comments, and "slower" students tend to offer more questions and responses (Tobin, 1987).

Provide Appropriate Assignments. As virtually every teacher knows, an assignment is the work students are assigned. Assignments can serve three purposes. First, assignments can enable students to learn. For example, an assignment that requires a student to locate and summarize five newspaper articles on President Clinton's health care plan enables students to learn more about that plan. Second, like questions, assignments permit teachers to check students' understanding; that is, once a teacher believes he or she has taught students to solve quadratic equations, he or she may give the students a worksheet that includes a dozen quadratic equations to solve. Students' performances on these worksheets provide the teacher with useful information about students' understanding of what they were taught about quadratic equations. Third, assignments can be used to promote retention and automaticity. *Retention* means that students will remember what they were taught, at least for the next day or two. *Automaticity* implies that students learn something so well that they no longer have to think about it. Examples of automaticity are learning to read, to play the piano, and to complete a double play in baseball. Automaticity frees the mind to concentrate on other things. Thus, for example, when automaticity has been achieved, reading becomes a means to an end, rather than an end in itself.

Unfortunately, the quality of many of the assignments given to students is questionable. Anderson (1987b) described "good" assignments as those (a) whose purpose and directions have been made clear to the students; (b) that are of "reasonable length"— long enough so that students can successfully complete them, yet short enough so that they are not perceived as busy work; and (c) that require students to "make or do" things that help keep them on task.

Provide Feedback to Students. Virtually all students want to know "how they're doing." Providing such information is known simply as "providing feedback." Feedback serves two primary purposes: (a) to reinforce appropriate student responses and (b) to correct inappropriate student responses. The latter type is often referred to as "corrective feedback." Finally, feedback may be positive (e.g., praise such as "Great job!"), negative (e.g., criticism such as "That answer shows that you're not thinking at all!"), or neutral (e.g, "Uh huh, OK").

Numerous researchers have found that reinforcing desired student behaviors increases the likelihood that students will repeat those behaviors. In fact, this principle lies at the heart of behavioral psychology. Effective teachers reinforce behaviors verbally by using brief phrases like "Nice job!", "Great answer!", or "Keep going. You're almost there!" Sometimes more powerful than verbal reinforcers, however, are nonverbal reinforcers, such as the physical messages sent by teachers through cues like eye contact, facial expression, and body position. Students pay close attention to whether the teacher smiles or frowns, whether the teacher looks at the student or avoids eye contact, and whether the teacher seems approachable or distant. By their verbal and nonverbal feedback to students, teachers either encourage or discourage student participation.

Corrective feedback is intended to provide students with cues about how their learning can be improved or their misunderstanding can be corrected. Once students respond to questions, they wait to have their answers validated. When the answers are incorrect, teachers have the opportunity to provide students with corrective feedback.

As with most instructional techniques, there is no single best approach to use when providing corrective feedback. The strategy most recommended, however, is prodding students. The teacher might rephrase the question or give the students hints or additional wait time. If these strategies are not successful and the teacher senses that the student does not know the correct answer or is becoming frustrated or embarrassed, the teacher should employ another strategy. For example, the teacher might state the correct answer or redirect the question to another student who may be able to provide the correct answer.

Summarizing the Lesson

At the end of each lesson, sometime before the bell rings or the students are otherwise excused, effective teachers summarize the lesson or provide *closure.* Shostak (1986) defined closure as the "skill of reviewing the key points of a lesson, of tying them together in a coherent whole, and finally, of ensuring their use by anchoring them in the student's larger conceptual framework" (p. 129). Closure serves three major purposes: (a) to draw attention to the end of a lesson or lesson segment; (b) to organize students' learning (to help them see the forest amidst the trees); and (c) to consolidate or reinforce the major points of the lesson.

If we were to bring closure to this chapter at this point in time, the following points would be made and emphasized.

- Effective teaching is a combination of both art and science.
- A key factor in a student's success is the level of his or her involvement in the learning process.
- Some of the major factors that influence a student's involvement in learning are (a) his or her level of physical and psychological comfort in the classroom and (b) the teacher's skill in teaching.
- Because teachers exercise considerable control over the physical and psychological environments in their classrooms, as well as over the quality of their teaching, they can significantly influence a student's level of involvement in learning.
- Typical lessons should consist of three steps if they are to be effective: (a) introducing the lesson, (b) explaining the lesson, and (c) summarizing the lesson.
- To increase the quality of their communication with students, teachers should (a) structure the lesson; (b) use examples and analogies; (c) use verbal cues; (d) address multiple learning modalities; (e) check for understanding; (f) provide appropriate assignments, and (g) provide feedback to students, suggesting ways students can improve their learning where necessary and appropriate.

Teacher Leaders
and Effective Teaching

During the past several decades, a great deal of knowledge has been added to the knowledge base of teaching. What can teacher leaders do to transmit this knowledge base to teachers and help them translate this knowledge base into action? The following three recommendations seem quite appropriate.

Promote a Collegial Environment in Schools

Making changes involves risk taking. Improvement demands change. Few people are willing to take the needed risks without some type of "safety net" beneath them. Teacher leaders can create such a net. Specifically, teacher leaders can help teachers understand that, like life, teaching is a development process. Perhaps the best treatment of the development of teacher expertise is that developed by Berliner (1994). Berliner suggested that teachers move through five stages as they progress from novices to experts: novice, advanced beginner, competency, proficiency, and expertise.

Providing an awareness of these stages for teachers does two things. First, it enables teachers to understand that they are always growing and developing as teachers. Thus, any mistakes they make or inadequacies they may have are best viewed as facilitating a transition to a higher stage of development. (Obviously, there are teachers who fixate at a given stage and whose mistakes simply reinforce the perception that they will stay at that stage indefinitely. Fortunately, such teachers are few in number.)

Second, an awareness of stages of development provides novice teachers the comfort of not feeling that they need to compete with the 20-year veteran. Furthermore, novice teachers may be helped to understand that they are not alone in their feelings; rather, numerous novice teachers are more concerned with personal survival than with the learning of their students. Similarly, many novice teachers have the greatest problems with classroom management.

Make the Knowledge Base of
Teaching Accessible to All Teachers

Far too many teachers truly believe that teaching is totally and completely an art; that is, they see no value in studying teaching or in discussing teaching problems with other teachers. Teacher leaders have the responsibility for helping their colleagues understand what Gage (1978) referred to as the "scientific basis of the art of teaching" (p. 13).

At the same time, however, it is important that teachers understand that research on effective teaching has not yielded a simple set of findings that, when implemented in classrooms, will guarantee increased effectiveness of teaching and learning. Rather, research on teaching has provided a conceptual framework for thinking about teaching and a common language for talking about thinking that will likely increase both understanding and effectiveness.

Several vehicles may be used for enhancing this understanding. Teacher leaders can work toward the publication of one-page (back and front) newsletters on current research and its application to practice. Teacher leaders also can be involved in the determination of perceived teacher needs (through some type of needs assessment) and the development of a comprehensive staff development program based on these needs. Finally, teacher leaders can arrange for times during which teachers can meet to discuss various teaching issues and problems. Often, teachers simply have a need to talk about things. At the present time, teachers have few opportunities to do so. "Saturday seminars" may be one way of providing such an opportunity. Unlike what their name implies, these seminars do not meet every Saturday; rather, they may meet the first Saturday of each month. Such seminars should have open agendas but should focus exclusively on the improvement of teaching.

Develop and Exhibit
Model Teaching Practices

Unfortunately, we talk to teachers about what they should do more than we demonstrate it. Numerous examples abound of how college professors of teacher education lecture about classroom discussion techniques. Teacher leaders not only need to "talk the talk"; they also need to "walk the walk."

Videotapes of real classes can be extremely useful. Videotapes permit teachers to see and hear what transpires during an excellent lesson. Split-screen videotapes, with the teacher on one half and the students on the other, are particularly useful in this regard.

In this way, the viewer can examine the reactions of students to various aspects of the lesson conducted by the teacher.

Modeling also is possible by inviting teachers into a teacher leader's classroom. In their classrooms, teacher leaders can display the ideas, strategies, and techniques that are being advocated at the present time. Quite obviously, these displays require a great deal of confidence on the part of teacher leaders. Questions about their strategies and techniques must not be perceived as threats; rather, they must be seen as opportunities for growth, both by the teachers and by the teacher leaders. Stated somewhat differently, insecurity does not breed teacher leaders.

Closing Comment

Although teaching involves certain elements of artistry, research findings indicate a scientific basis for the art of teaching. The results of numerous studies suggest that perhaps the primary factor in a student's success is his or her involvement in the learning process. The role of the teacher, then, is to promote and enhance student involvement. Teachers have considerable control over many of the factors that affect student involvement in learning. Among the most important of these factors are the classroom's physical environment, the psychological tone of the classroom, and the quality of the communication between teacher and student. The way in which teachers choose to operate with respect to these factors will significantly affect students' attitudes, behaviors, and achievement.

6

Helping Teachers Learn From Their Students

There is no doubt that students have much to learn from their teachers. The major thesis of this chapter is that teachers have much to learn from their students. To be successful, in fact, teachers must attend to what their students do, what they say, and how they perform.

The primary purpose of this chapter is to explore ways in which teachers can learn from their students. A secondary purpose is to examine how teachers, individually and collectively, can use what they learn from their students to improve their teaching. To accomplish these two purposes, the chapter is organized into seven sections.

We begin with a discussion of various definitions of teaching, suggesting that definitions that exclude learning are inappropriate. The next three sections describe three sources of information from students that teachers currently have available to them: students' classroom behavior, students' responses to classroom questions, and students' performance on in-class assignments, homework, quizzes, and tests. The fifth section includes a brief discussion of the reluctance of teachers to learn from their students. The sixth section discusses the importance of teacher leadership. The last section contains a set of recommendations for teacher leaders in helping teachers learn from their students.

What Is Teaching?

Teaching has many definitions. The simplest ones are fairly circular and very behavioral: Teaching is what teachers do. On the basis of these definitions, explaining complex issues to students, disciplining students for their misbehavior, grading students' papers, or wiping the sweat off one's brow as one struggles to get a point across to a reticent student are all acts of teaching.

Other definitions add a *normative* dimension. Are teachers doing what they *should* be doing? Obviously, normative definitions require that someone define the "shoulds." Most typically, they are derived from cultural values and educational philosophies. Normative definitions enable one to differentiate, for example, acts of teaching from those of brainwashing. Sometimes individual educators contribute their own values to normative definitions of teaching, as the following story illustrates.

One of us (Anderson) was conducting an observational study in a number of middle school classrooms. In one of these classrooms, the teacher had her students engaged in cooperative learning. It just happened that, on this particular day, the principal of the school had scheduled a formal evaluation of this teacher. He entered the room, nodded to the teacher, sat in the back of the classroom, and began to observe. After about 5 minutes, he rose from his chair, went up to the teacher, and whispered in her ear, "I'll come back when you are teaching." Quite clearly, what the teacher was doing did not meet the principal's normative definition of teaching.

Still other definitions add *intention* to the behavioral definition of teaching; that is, teaching is what teachers do when they intend to facilitate or foster learning on the part of their students. According to these definitions, explaining complex issues to students is definitely an act of teaching, whereas disciplining students for their misbehavior or grading students' papers is less likely to be.

Finally, some definitions rely on learning to define teaching. On the basis of these definitions, teaching not only requires intention on the part of the teacher but also requires learning on the part of the students. Smith (1987) referred to these definitions as "effectiveness" definitions. To paraphrase an aged scientific problem, "If a teacher gave a brilliant lecture to a group of students but none of the students learned anything, was the teacher teaching?" In the context of effectiveness definitions, the answer is a resounding No!

Our definition of teaching is some combination of the *normative* and *effectiveness* definitions. We reject the *behavioral* definition out of hand. In this regard, we agree with Jackson (1986), who wrote:

> There is no such thing as a behavioral definition of teaching and there never can be. We can never simply watch a person in action and be sure that something called teaching is going on. . . . Our attempt to say when a person is or is not teaching is always an act of interpretation. We are forever "readers" of human action, seeking to determine which "reading" is correct from among those possible. (pp. 77-78)

Furthermore, we believe that the *intentional* definition, though a good start, does not go far enough. We are reminded, uncomfortably, by the old proverb, "The road to Hell is paved with good intentions."

Normative definitions define the boundaries within which teaching can be said to occur. More specifically, they define acts and behaviors that lie outside these boundaries. Stated somewhat differently, normative definitions highlight the moral dimension of teaching. Thus, in our culture, brainwashing is "out of bounds."

A normative definition of teaching, as well as an effectiveness definition, is needed. Teaching without learning is an empty act. It is "going through the motions." It places undue emphasis on the teacher. It undervalues the student. Stated simply, an effectiveness definition of teaching prohibits a teacher from assuming that he or she has taught something to some student or group of students;

rather, it requires that the teacher seek out evidence of students' learning.

Teachers can use three sources of evidence as they attempt to determine whether they indeed have taught their students: (a) They can observe students' reactions in class; (b) they can ask questions of their students and encourage their students to ask questions of them; and (c) they can examine a variety of students' products (e.g., homework assignments, standardized test results).

Classroom Observations

Numerous research studies have confirmed teachers' use of students' reactions to determine whether they are "getting across" to their students (Dahloff, 1971; Jackson, 1968). In fact, Jackson contended that teachers judge their effectiveness more on the basis of students' behavior than on achievement. Teachers rely on a variety of "signals" from their students. "Eyes on" behavior means students are "with you." Squirming behavior means they are tired or bored. Affirmative nods of the head mean they understand; puzzled looks mean they are confused.

In large classrooms, teachers cannot monitor all students all of the time. As a consequence, many teachers focus on small groups of students, called "steering groups." Members of a steering group may be chosen because of where they sit in the classroom (Lambert, 1994) or because of their academic standing (Torper, 1994).

The major decision that teachers make on the basis of their observations of students is when it is appropriate to move on to the next topic, point, problem, or issue. Thus, steering groups control the pace at which instruction occurs. The more academically able the students in the steering group, the more rapid the pace, and conversely.

Not all teachers rely on students' reactions to make pacing decisions. Some teachers are "clock (or calendar) watchers" more than "student watchers." These teachers feel compelled to cover a certain amount of material within a given time period. In this regard, one of us (Anderson) is reminded of a mathematics teacher he encountered many years ago when objectives were the hot topic in education. He asked the mathematics teacher what his major goal was for his algebra students; the teacher replied, "To get to the quadratic equation by Easter." He then asked, "How many of your students will get there with you?" The teacher responded, "About a third."

Observations of students' reactions do provide teachers with some information concerning the effectiveness of their teaching. At the same time, however, it must pointed out that using this source has some problems. Observations provide more information about students' attentiveness than students' learning. Although a relationship between attentiveness and learning exists, the two terms are not synonymous. Because of the number of students in most classrooms, not all students can be observed all of the time. Thus, teachers tend to focus on certain students and not others. The extent to which the "readings" that teachers make of these students are generalizable to the class as a whole is not known. Finally, some teachers are better "readers" of their students than are others. (Some teachers apparently do not even "open the book.") Thus, although observations may provide very useful information for the first group of teachers, they may be misleading or irrelevant for others.

Unfortunately, observations, like most data collection activities, take time. In economic terms, they are labor intensive. Fortunately, videotapes can be used to make records of teachers teaching. Once a videotape of a lesson has been made, teacher leaders can sit with teachers to review and discuss various aspects of the lesson that went well or were problematic. Videotaped lessons also provide an opportunity for self-reflection.

Obviously, not all lessons can be videotaped. Videotaping three or four lessons each term or each year, however, is likely to be very instructive.

Classroom Questions

In addition to reading students' reactions in the classroom, teachers can ask questions of their students to check the level of understanding. They also can respond to questions raised by their students. Fortunately, much is known about questioning as a way of classroom life (Anderson, 1994).

First, teachers ask many questions. On average, teachers in their classrooms ask almost one question every minute. Surprisingly, many of these questions do not require answers from the students. Some are rhetorical: "Have you ever wondered how it is that large ships made of iron can float?" Others require nods, rather than verbal responses: "Yesterday, we discussed the first act of *Macbeth*. Right?"

Second, of those questions that require students' answers, most require very short ones: "Jermaine, can you name two functions of the fibula?" "Who can tell me the name of the United States president who was in office during the start of the Vietnam War?" "Rosita, what is the slope of the line in Figure 1?" Rarely are extended or expanded answers from students required.

Third, as most of the above questions illustrate, the vast majority of questions asked by teachers require students to recall previously taught information or material. Our best estimates indicate that fewer than one of every four questions requires some form of thought on the part of students (Anderson & Sosniak, 1994; Goodlad, 1984).

Fourth, and likely related to the previous point, teachers do not wait very long for students to respond to the questions they are asked. Wait times of 1 or 2 seconds are quite common. Given the nature of the questions asked, however, this amount of wait time is not necessarily inappropriate. Either students know the answers, or they do not. When questions requiring higher order thinking are asked, however, the evidence suggests that increased wait time (even allowing just 4 or 5 seconds) is necessary and beneficial (Tobin, 1987). Furthermore, asking the question to the entire class, allowing appropriate wait time, and then calling on a student is likely to engage all students in the thought process needed to answer the question being asked.

Fifth, students ask questions of teachers very rarely. In contrast to the 1-per-minute rate of teacher questioning, it has been estimated that the typical student asks a question of the teacher approximately once each month (Berliner, 1988). This paucity of student questioning may result from a lack of opportunity to ask questions or the influence of peer pressure. For many students, admitting ignorance is a "badge of dishonor" (Jackson, 1988). For these students, it is better in the eyes of their peers for their ignorance to go unchecked.

Like observations of students' reactions, classroom questions are a potentially useful source of information to teachers concerning their effectiveness. Also like observations, several problems are associated with classroom questions. First, too many of the questions asked by teachers focus more on memorization than on meaning. Thus, in too many cases, teachers are left with a vague understanding of their students' understanding. Second, students are given too little time to think before responding to teachers' questions. Thus, not only do these questions focus on memorization, but they also emphasize instantaneous recall. Third, students' questions, perhaps the best source for teachers to gauge students' levels of understanding during the teaching process, are very infrequent. Finding ways to encourage questions and to convey the fact that questions are expected remains a challenge for most teachers.

As in the case of observations, collecting data on classroom questions can be time-consuming. Fortunately, however, questions are oral; that is, they can be recorded with audiotapes. Like videotapes, audiotapes provide a permanent record of classroom transactions. Unlike videotapes, however, they are less obtrusive. Audiotapes can be made by placing an audiotape recorder on the teacher's desk or some central classroom location and turning it on. Once an audiotape is made, it can be reviewed by the teacher or by the teacher along with a lead teacher or other relevant person.

Assignments, Quizzes, and Teacher-Made Tests

Teachers also can learn about the effectiveness of their teaching by examining their students' performances on assignments (both in-class and at-home), quizzes, and tests. Interestingly, this tremendous amount of information is rarely used by teachers for this purpose; rather, teachers use assignments, quizzes, and tests to evaluate the amount and quality of their students' learning, not the quality of their teaching.

This emphasis on learning, rather than on teaching, is particularly striking because assignments, quizzes, and tests provide information on both. It just depends on how one looks at the data obtained from these measures. To understand this assertion, one must examine the structure of assignments, quizzes, and tests in relation to the students who take them.

All assignments, quizzes, and tests contain a set of tasks to which students are expected to respond. These tasks may be questions, exercises, problems, or test items. Most often, the expected response to a given task is written; at other times, it may be oral or behavioral.

Tasks place demands on students in terms of the knowledge and/or skill they need to complete them. On the one hand, if the demand is too great, the student fails to accomplish the task: The student answers a question incorrectly, produces a faulty or incomplete solution to a problem, or, in testing terminology, is "wrong." On the other hand, if the knowledge and/or skill possessed by the student is extensive, the student accomplishes the task: He or she gives a correct answer to the question, solves the problem, or, again in testing terminology, is "right."

Thus, assignments, quizzes, and tests can best be understood as a conflict between a student and a set of tasks. If the tasks demand more than the student can deliver, the result is failure. If the tasks demand less than the student can deliver, success follows. A visual display of the results of one such conflict is shown in Table 6.1.

The rows of Table 6.1 include 10 students, labeled A through J. The columns of the table correspond with 10 tasks given to these students (1 through 10). The entries in the cells of the table, 0's or 1's, indicate the "winner" of the conflict. A 1 means the student was victorious; he or she completed the task successfully. In contrast, a 0 means the task was victorious; the student went down to defeat.

TABLE 6.1   A Summary of the "Conflict" Between Students
and Tasks

Student	Topic I			+	Topic II		+	Topic III			Total
	1	2	3	4	5	6	7	8	9	10	Total
A	1	1	0	0	0	0	1	0	0	1	4
B	1	1	1	1	1	1	1	1	1	1	10
C	1	1	1	0	1	0	1	0	1	1	7
D	1	1	0	0	0	0	0	1	1	1	5
E	1	1	1	0	0	0	1	0	1	0	5
F	1	1	1	0	1	0	1	1	1	1	8
G	1	1	1	0	0	0	0	0	0	0	3
H	1	0	1	1	1	1	1	1	1	1	9
I	1	1	1	0	0	0	1	1	0	1	6
J	1	1	1	0	0	1	1	1	1	1	8
Total	10	9	8	2	4	3	8	6	7	8	65

NOTE: Students G and A did more poorly than the rest; Tasks 4 and 6 were
more difficult than the rest.

It is important to note that the numbers in the cells of the table
can be combined in two ways. First, the numbers can be added
within each row. This summation focuses on the performance of
each student. Thus, for example, it can be seen that Student A had
a total score of 4, whereas Student B had a total score of 10.
Teachers tend to look at the results of the conflict in this way; they
want to know which students learned well and which did not.
They often assign grades to students on the basis of this examination of the table.

Second, the numbers in the cells can be added within each
column. This summation focuses on the difficulty of each task.
When the column sums are examined, for example, it can be seen
that Task 1 was completed successfully by all 10 students, whereas
Task 4 was completed successfully by only 2. If the assumption is

made that the teacher tried equally hard to teach the knowledge and skills related to both tasks *and* if the task is well conceived and presented to the student in a way he or she can understand it, one can conclude that the teacher did a much better job on Task 1 than on Task 4. Looking at the column totals, rather than the row totals, then, provides information about the quality of teaching rather than the quality of learning.

Well-written assignments, quizzes, and tests organize the tasks around important objectives, skills, competencies, or topics. For the purpose of discussion, we use the term *topic* to represent these possible "organizers." As can be seen in Table 6.1, the 10 tasks are related to three topics: I, II, and III. This relationship of tasks to topics permits an examination of the quality of teaching beyond the individual task. In the example, students did much better on the tasks related to Topic I than they did on the tasks related to Topic II. Their performance on the tasks related to Topic III was somewhere between these two extremes. Again, assuming that the teacher "cared" equally about all three topics, one can conclude that the quality of teaching relative to Topic I was better than that for Topic II. Depending on the importance attached to Topic II, then, the teacher may decide to spend some additional time and effort on it.

Students' performances on assignments, quizzes, and teacher-made tests provide a third source of evidence for teachers. Like the previous two sources, however, the use of these data is not without problems. First, some tasks are more complex than others. Multistage problems are more complex than single-stage problems. Inferring a main idea is more complex than recognizing an explicitly stated main idea. More complex tasks are generally more difficult than less complex tasks regardless of the quality of teaching. Second, the way a task is presented to students may influence its difficulty. Confusing directions, a lack of directions, inappropriate vocabulary, overly complex statements—all of these factors increase the difficulty of a task regardless of actual complexity of the task. Thus, poor student performance on tasks does not always speak to the quality of teaching received by the student. At the same time, however, teachers who ignore data from students' assignments, quizzes, and classroom tests are missing a tremendous opportunity to learn about their teaching effectiveness.

Teacher leaders need to understand the impact that assignments, quizzes, and tests have on both teachers and students. Assignments and quizzes often communicate to students what is really important. Tests, especially standardized ones, which we discuss in the next section, are things that teacher should teach toward. We can argue that assignments should not be as important to students as they are and that teachers should not "teach the test." However, a more productive approach is to ensure that the assignments given by teachers are meaningful and relevant and that the items included on tests represent what is important for students to learn. This is a primary role of teacher leaders.

Standardized Tests

Standardized tests are simply a special case of tests in general. The term *standardized* means that all students receive tests that include an identical set of tasks, are expected to respond to these tasks in the same way (e.g., selecting from options, writing short answers), and are administered the tests under uniform conditions (a common set of directions and time limits). Virtually everything written in the previous section applies to standardized tests.

Standardized tests do pose some unique problems, however. First, not all of the tasks included on these tests are equally valid for all students; that is, not all students may have had an opportunity to learn the knowledge or skill needed to perform the task correctly (e.g., answer the question, solve the problem). Second, not all response formats are equally appropriate for all students. For example, some students have difficulty with multiple-choice formats but can perform well when allowed to write out their responses. Third, uniform administrative conditions imply uniform students. Quite obviously, time limits are too stringent for some students and too liberal for others.

An additional problem stems from the primary way the results of standardized tests are reported and, hence, understood by most teachers. The emphasis in reporting standardized test results is on individual students—specifically, the performance of individual students relative to the total population. Thus, for example, say that Stone Hardaway's score on *A Total Test of Applied Conceptual Knowledge* (ATTACK) places him at or above 83% of his peers who took the test at the same time. One then can say that Stone is at the 83rd percentile. One can conclude further that his score places him in the upper quarter of those tested.

To summarize the performance of students on standardized tests, they typically are divided into four subgroups called "quarters." Then one can talk about the percentage of students who are in the first, second, third, and fourth quarters. Some educators confuse "quarters" with "quartiles." They say, for example, that Stone Hardaway is in the "upper quartile." This is incorrect because the quartile is the dividing point between quarters. Thus, although there are only three quartiles (which correspond with the 25th, 50th, and 75th percentiles), there are four quarters.

Educators whose knowledge of standardized test results is limited to individual student performance, percentiles, quartiles, and quarters are often surprised to learn that the publishers of most standardized tests also provide what are termed "right-response" summaries. A right-response summary is a printout of the percentage of students who answered each item correctly (see Table 6.2). These right-response summaries tend to be organized by topic or objective and thus offer an opportunity to begin to examine the quality of teaching provided by the teacher on each topic or objective.

To make sense of these right-response summaries, it seems reasonable to group them (like students) into quarters. The first (lowest) quarter would include those items (tasks) that were the most difficult. By "difficult," we mean those items that the *fewest* students answered correctly. The fourth (upper) quarter would include the items (tasks) that were the easiest. Items in this quarter would be those that the *most* students answered correctly. The transformation of the right-response summaries into "quarters" is shown in Table 6.3.

Once summaries are grouped in this fashion, a series of questions can be asked about the data. First, are particular topics or

TABLE 6.2 Portion of a Right-Response Summary

Item	Description	Percentage Correct
IN1	Make a comparison based on information in a selection	64.8
IN2	Identify the cause of an event described in a selection	83.0
IN3	Identify the effect of an event described in a selection	61.4
IN4	Draw an appropriate conclusion based on information in a selection	68.9
IN5	Draw an appropriate conclusion based on information in a selection	61.7
IN6	Predict an outcome based on information in a selection	79.8
IN7	Analyze a selection to identify a structural element—plot	54.8
IN8	Analyze a selection to identify a rhetorical device—metaphor	74.5

TABLE 6.3 Right-Response Summaries Divided Into Quarters

Difficulties	Item/Description		Percentage Correct
Easiest	IN2	Identify cause of an event	83.0
	IN6	Predict outcome	79.8
2nd Quarter	IN8	Analyze selection—metaphor	74.5
	IN4	Draw appropriate conclusion	68.9
3rd Quarter	IN1	Make comparison	64.8
	IN5	Draw appropriate conclusion	61.7
Most difficult	IN3	Identify effect of an event	61.4
	IN7	Analyze selection—plot	54.8

SOURCE: Adapted from 1994 South Carolina Basic Skills Assessment Program summaries.

objectives overly represented in the first (lowest) quarter? In Table 6.3, one can see that questions dealing with "outcomes" (e.g., conclusions, effects) are more difficult than those dealing with "inputs" (e.g., causes, predictions). Thus, the teacher should determine whether these differences are important, whether they reflect the emphasis given to them, and whether he or she should make changes in curriculum and/or instruction. If, in contrast to Table 6.3, the topics and objectives are fairly randomly distributed among the quarters, no additional analysis is needed.

Second, if any topics and objectives are overly represented in the lowest quarter, are they important in the overall scheme of things? If they are not important, there is nothing to worry about; students apparently are having difficulty with trivial tasks.

Third, if the topics and objectives are important, are they emphasized in class? If they are not, should they be? The answer to this question requires some soul searching, either individually or collectively. If the topics and objectives are emphasized and students still are performing poorly on the tasks related to these topics and objectives, a major problem has been identified. This problem leads to our final question: What can be done to improve the quality of instruction provided to students on these topics and objectives?

It must be recognized that the examination of right-response summaries takes time. Middle school and high school teachers having the responsibility for approximately 150 students certainly will not wish to engage in this activity for every assignment or test. Nonetheless, by sharing the workload on standardized tests with other teachers and by selecting specific assignments to review, teachers can learn a great deal from the way their students respond to the various tasks they are assigned. As has been mentioned throughout this volume, finding time for teachers to engage in activities such as this is a major problem confronting teacher leaders.

Despite the many problems associated with standardized tests, the information they provide can be used by teachers to examine and, perhaps, improve their teaching. To reject such tests out of hand is a mistake made by far too many teachers.

The Reluctance of Teachers
to Learn From Their Students

As the previous discussion indicates, teachers can learn much from their students—their classroom behaviors, their responses to questions, the questions they ask, their performance on classroom assignments and quizzes, and their scores on standardized tests. In fact, it is precisely what teachers learn from their students that enables them to become better teachers.

Nonetheless, many teachers are reluctant to learn from their students. Although many reasons can be given for this reluctance, four reasons seem to stand out: (a) teachers' roles in their classrooms, (b) teachers' relationships with their students, (c) teachers' fear of evaluation, and (d) teachers' lack of awareness of the data available to them.

Teachers' Roles in Classrooms

Teachers can assume a variety of roles in their classrooms. They can be the sole source of knowledge, or they can be a facilitator of student learning. They can operate from the belief that absolute truth exists or from the belief that students construct their own reality. In the vernacular, they can be a "sage on the stage" or a "guide on the side."

Teachers who are "sole sources" and "truth givers" believe that their students learn from them. As a consequence, the only thing these teachers can learn from their students is whether or not the desired learning has occurred. For these teachers, the failure of students to learn is typically the students' fault (either because of their lack of ability or their home background). Rarely do these teachers ask what they can do to improve their students' learning. After all, some students "have it," and others simply do not. Thus, for these teachers, the possibility of learning from their students is rejected out of hand.

In contrast, teachers who believe they are primarily responsible for creating the conditions that likely will lead to learning on the part of their students typically seek out and value feedback from students because this feedback lets them know whether these conditions have been created. In addition, this feedback helps the teachers understand for which students the conditions have been conducive to learning and for which students they have not.

Teachers' Relationships
With Their Students

Teachers can establish a number of different relationships with their students. Teachers and students can exist in a superordinate-subordinate relationship. In this situation, teachers are the "bosses" and students are the "workers." Teachers are the "lords of the manor" and students are the "serfs." (Perhaps that's why some California students would rather be "serfing" than in school.)

Or, teachers and students can exist in a mutually supportive, symbiotic relationship. In this situation, teachers are aware that they need students, and students are aware that they need teachers. The concepts of "mutual respect" and "we are all in this together" govern what takes place in classrooms.

Although in the former teacher-student relationship, students are a threat to a teacher's power and authority, in the latter relationship, teachers and students learn from one another. Mistakes are made on both sides, and only by finding ways of correcting these mistakes can both groups benefit.

Evaluation Phobia

Evaluation phobia occurs when teachers believe that any information obtained from their students can only be used against them. These teachers fear that administrators will use student data only to determine "good" and "poor" teachers. Evaluation phobia is especially acute when a teacher further believes that he or she falls into the "poor" teacher category. In addition, the more data that administrators gather, the more likely it is they are trying to "get someone." After all, everyone knows that additional information is needed if a teacher is to be reprimanded or terminated. Administrators collect data simply to support their case against a teacher.

Unfortunately, we have been in schools and school districts in which this phobia is well grounded. Administrators *do* attempt to "get the goods" on poor teachers. Additional classroom observations and other documentation *do* mean someone's job is in danger. It is quite sad when data are used only for negative purposes. This practice creates an environment in which data are to be avoided at all costs. Such an environment is antithetical to the propositions offered in this chapter.

Lack of Awareness

Finally, many teachers want to learn from their students but just don't know how to do it. They do not recognize the value of developing a reliable steering group. They do not understand the importance of establishing an environment conducive to student questioning. They do not realize that information about both teaching and learning is embedded in students' performances on assignments, quizzes, and tests. For most of these teachers, increasing their awareness may be sufficient for improving their teaching.

Importance of Teacher Leadership in Learning From Students

Overcoming the reluctance that teachers have about learning from their students requires teacher leadership. In some schools, administrators cannot provide this leadership because they are perceived as "the enemy." In other schools, administrators are either unwilling or unable to do so.

Teachers as colleagues offer several support services not available from other sources. First, issues concerning the proper role of the teacher in facilitating students' learning are best addressed in an open, supportive environment. Teachers cannot be told to become more facilitative and nurturing; rather, they must be helped to understand that teachers who serve as "guides on the side" not only are more effective but also are more satisfied with the job of teaching. Helping teachers to understand this new role requires open discussions with other teachers and opportunities to visit other teachers' classrooms.

Second, the use of information provided by students to understand and improve one's teaching is alien to many teachers. Appropriate instruments to collect such information may need to be developed, the meaning of the information may need to be discussed, and conditions that enable teachers to have the confidence needed to learn from this information may need to be created. Once again, teachers must take the lead in creating such conditions.

Third, problems associated with teacher effectiveness are best discussed with other teachers. It is extremely difficult to admit to one's faults in the presence of supervisors, particularly those who do not have one's best interests in mind. Furthermore, teachers who have experienced such problems and difficulties are quite likely to have strategies they have used to attack these problems and difficulties in the past.

What Teacher Leaders Can Do

Teacher leaders can do several things to help teachers learn from their students. Some of these things require working with groups of teachers; others can be done with individual teachers.

First, teacher leaders can prepare one-page "infograms" for distribution to teachers. An infogram summarizes a particular topic or issue and suggests ways in which teachers can implement the topic or resolve the issue. An example of an infogram for the creation of an "inquiry environment" is shown in Figure 6.1. Infograms also can be prepared for the formation and use of steering groups and the interpretation and use of right-response summaries. Infograms can be used to provide ongoing staff development for teachers.

Second, teacher leaders can develop or identify instruments that can aid teachers in obtaining information for improving their effectiveness in the classroom. Some of these instruments may re-

Creating an Inquiry Environment

In many subject areas, the questions asked are at least equally important as the answers given. Subjects such as science and social studies particularly lend themselves to being taught within an "inquiry environment." Inquiry environments are characterized by questions, dialogue (rather than lecture), and informed opinions (as well as facts). Inquiry environments enable teachers to learn much about what and how students think, as well as about the misinformation and misunderstandings they possess.

Teachers can create inquiry environments by attending to and implementing the following suggestions.

1. Teachers can serve as models of inquiry; that is, they can ask thoughtful, meaningful questions as they introduce topics or ideas. They can inform students of the questions with which they have struggled (and perhaps continue to struggle) as they attempt to understand and explain a particular topic or idea.

2. Teachers can create classrooms in which questions from students are not only encouraged but also *expected.* Simply rewording the typical questions that teachers ask their students goes a long way in this regard.

Typical question	*Better question*
A. Does anyone have any questions?	A. Who has the first question today?
B. What are the three major points made by the author?	B. What are the three assumptions being made by the author?
C. Jamal, can you tell me something about King Claudius?	C. Jamal, what person do you know who is most like King Claudius? Describe him or her for me.

In addition, students can be given assignments that require them to raise questions about topics and ideas, to write them down, and to be prepared to ask and discuss them in class.

3. Teachers can communicate to students that they value the students' answers and opinions. One easy way to do this is to increase the time that the teacher waits for students to answer the questions he or she asks. The fairly typical 1- or 2-second wait time can be increased to 3, 4, or 5 seconds. Furthermore, teachers can work continuously to improve their listening skills.

Figure 6.1. Infogram on Creating an Inquiry Environment

quire that teachers reflect on their current practices; others may require that students respond to a series of questions or statements.

An example of the first type is shown in Figure 6.2, The Academic Work Checklist. This instrument is useful in helping teachers critically examine the assignments they give their students.
The periodic use of an instrument like this one enables teachers to
monitor the quality of their assignments. Higher quality assignments yield higher quality information from students.

An example of the second type—instruments completed by
students—is displayed in Figure 6.3, Student Feedback Form. It
gives teachers information concerning how well a particular lesson "went" from their students' point of view. Instruments like
this one should not be overused, or else students may find them
tedious and respond to them capriciously. At the same time, the
use of such instruments once or twice a month may provide
teachers with insights they would not otherwise have.

Third, teacher leaders can arrange for teacher task forces to
study important issues. One key issue is the alignment between
what is being taught and what is included on standardized tests.
The format shown in Figure 6.2 can be used to analyze selected
classrooms. Based on these analyses, curricular decisions such as
moving topics from grade level to grade level and increasing the
emphasis of specific topics at particular grade levels can be made.
In addition, policy papers that educate school board members,
business leaders, and the general public concerning the relationship of standardized tests to the approved curriculum can be
written and distributed.

Finally, teacher leaders can work with administrators to create
an atmosphere in which information gathered from students is used
to make instructional decisions. In too many schools today, information is power. To paraphrase Popham (1982), in an information-
based enterprise, those who control the information control the
enterprise. The education community must move away from this
view that information is something to be hoarded and tucked
away, brought out only to promote one's point of view or to justify
a decision made or a position taken, and teachers must lead this
movement. All teachers need to be constantly aware of how well
their students, individually and collectively, are learning. Without

The Academic Work Checklist

Directions: Select an assignment you have given your students.
Analyze it in terms of the following six questions by circling the proper
response. The greater the number of "no" and "not sure" responses, the
lower the quality of the assignment. Relevant comments pertaining to
each question can be made on the reverse side.

	Response *(Circle one)*
Question	
1. Is the purpose of the assignment clear to the students; that is, do they know what is being learned, practiced, or assessed?	Yes No Not sure
2. Will completion of the assignment likely result in the students accomplishing the intended purpose?	Yes No Not sure
3. Is the assignment organized in a way that enables students to complete it successfully? (Assignments may be organized by topic, format, difficulty, etc.)	Yes No Not sure
4. Is the length of the assignment reasonable in view of the intended purpose and available time?	Yes No Not sure
5. Are directions for completing the assignment clearly stated, preferably in writing?	Yes No Not sure
6. Are the criteria and standards that are used to judge the quality of the students' work or performance explicit and clear, that is, do students know how their work or performance will be evaluated?	Yes No Not sure

Figure 6.2. How Good Are the Assignments You Give Your Students?
SOURCE: Adapted from *Increasing Teacher Effectiveness* (pp. 99-100), by
L. W. Anderson, 1991, Paris, France: UNESCO International Institute for
Educational Planning.

such information, teachers have no choice but to rely on tradition,
intuition, and their own unique belief systems as they struggle to
survive and improve. If teachers do not learn from their students,
students quite likely will not learn from their teachers.

Student Feedback Form

Directions: To help you learn better, I need your feedback. Read carefully each of the first nine statements below. If you agree with the statement, circle the word *yes*. If you disagree, circle the word *no*. If you are unsure about whether you agree or disagree, circle *not sure*. The final two statements ask you to provide written comments. Write as much as you feel the need to write. Use the back of this sheet if necessary. You do not need to write your name on this paper. Thanks for your input!

Statements	*Responses* *(Circle one)*
1. The teacher told me what I was expected to learn today.	Yes No Not sure
2. It was easy for me to understand the teacher's explanations.	Yes No Not sure
3. I felt comfortable asking questions in class.	Yes No Not sure
4. The teacher called on me at least once during the class period.	Yes No Not sure
5. I had an opportunity in class to practice what I was learning.	Yes No Not sure
6. Little time was wasted during class.	Yes No Not sure
7. The teacher reviewed the main points at the end of class.	Yes No Not sure
8. I learned a lot today in this class.	Yes No Not sure
9. I enjoyed this class today.	Yes No Not sure

10. My teacher helps me learn by _____
    _____
    _____

11. My teacher could help me learn better if he or she _____
    _____
    _____

Figure 6.3. Student Feedback Form

PART THREE

Teachers Working Together to Reclaim Schools

7

Helping Teachers Grow Professionally

Becoming a professional teacher is a journey, not a destination. No teacher springs from the head of Zeus as a full-blown professional. To appreciate this, all teachers need only relive in their memories that first week on the job to feel once again the knot in the pit of the stomach that was their constant companion on the too-short drive to school. If further proof is needed, they need only recall the fear they felt every minute of those first few days and weeks. In their heart of hearts, they were deathly afraid that the children would see through their bravado and sense their deepest, most carefully guarded secret; that they were fearful that they might not even survive the school year, much less teach the children what they needed to know.

Fortunately, experience and additional training through participation in staff development programs eventually calmed the fears and assuaged the doubts of most teachers. As they gained experience and developed their teaching skills, they became more comfortable in the knowledge that they could effectively control their own destinies and perhaps even make a worthwhile contribution to the lives of the children entrusted to their care.

Historically, the focus of staff development has been on correcting teacher deficiencies. This may have something to do with the fact that most, if not all, teachers start out with more deficiencies than most teachers care to admit. There is no shame in starting a teaching career in a deficient state; teaching is an extremely complex profession, requiring extensive training and practice before a reasonable level of proficiency can be attained. The real shame, however, is that the complexity of the teaching profession, which makes the transition from training to practice so difficult, may have unduly influenced the fundamental nature of staff development programs for teachers, causing those programs to be ineffective for teachers who are beyond the novice stage of their careers.

Until quite recently, staff development commonly was referred to in the professional literature as "inservice education," perhaps connoting the universally held belief that all teachers are defective to one degree or another. Because educators have long been accustomed to operating staff development programs from a deficiency model, teachers quite naturally have associated negative feelings with inservice education. Inservice education has been something that was done *to* teachers, not with teachers or by teachers *for* teachers. Not surprisingly, some teachers have openly expressed their resentment at "being inserviced." Even more significantly, countless others have passively resisted the efforts directed toward "inservicing" them. This passive resistance has been reflected in their grumbling and complaining, in their expressed lack of interest in the programs that have been offered to them, and most eloquently, through their stoic determination not to be influenced by the mountain of inservice education to which they are routinely subjected against their will.

Sadly, teachers have good reason to be dissatisfied with most of the staff development they have experienced over the years. Although the professed goals of staff development have been to positively influence teachers' beliefs, attitudes, and instructional practices in order to improve students' learning outcomes (Griffin, 1983), the de facto goals have been cost effectiveness and efficiency. Evidence to support this conclusion is reflected in the fact that, for the most part, teacher inservice programs historically have been severely underfunded (Cooper, 1994; Wagner, 1994).

The marginal financial commitment to promoting substantial professional growth for teachers during a career has fostered the most common approach to delivering staff development: the "one-shot" workshop. By attempting to deal with the complexities of teaching as if they could be understood and mastered at a single sitting, the education profession has effectively devalued teaching and, at the same time, turned off millions of teachers to the potential opportunities that exist for personal and professional growth through inservice education.

In the name of expediency, teachers also have been effectively excluded from any meaningful participation in planning and implementing staff development programs. Little effort has been expended to adequately assess and prioritize staff development needs at the district, school, or individual levels. Furthermore, teachers' preferences have not been considered seriously in determining how, when, and where staff development programs will be delivered. Teachers routinely have been expected to participate in staff development activities on their own time. Released time for staff development for teachers has been regarded as *paid time off*, an undeserved perk. All of these points have translated into staff development programs that do not remotely meet the needs or interests of a great majority of teachers. Is it any wonder that teachers have been so reticent to embrace staff development?

Within the past few years, the issues surrounding staff development have attracted renewed interest, and for several very important reasons. One reason is the realization that people are the most important resource available to school districts as they seek to accomplish their missions. Material, equipment, and supplies comprise a relatively small portion of the operating budgets of most school districts. In fact, it is generally well known that more than two thirds of district operating budgets are devoted to wages and salaries. Therefore, it behooves those in positions to establish policy to allocate sufficient resources to ensure the adequate development of the most important resource of any school district—its people.

A second reason that staff development has recently assumed a more important position in the pecking order of school district priorities is that fewer talented students are selecting teacher training in their college preparation programs (Darling-Hammond, 1984). The result is that, for the foreseeable future, fewer highly trained and highly skilled new teachers will be available to school districts throughout the country. School districts, therefore, will have to make do with those teachers already in the teaching force. For better or for worse, significant improvement in instructional programs and services will be tied directly to how successful school districts are in helping those teachers already in the system further refine and develop their professional knowledge and skills.

A third reason for a renewed emphasis on staff development is the growing interest of a critical mass of people, both inside and outside the education community, in restructuring the nation's schools. The growing realization among all of those who care about this nation's future is that something must be done to fundamentally reshape schools in order to make them more effective and, thereby, more productive. Many people are convinced that reshaping schools can best be accomplished by better using the largely untapped resources that exist in all of our schools for dynamic new kinds of teacher leadership. Staff development is the key to unleashing this powerful resource.

A fourth reason that staff development is becoming more critical to the ultimate effectiveness of schools is related to the increasing numbers of teachers being recruited from fields other than education. In most cases, these new recruits, although they may be strong in content, have no real knowledge of teaching pedagogy. For the most part, they get only crash courses in teaching, with the primary emphasis on classroom control and management. If they ultimately are to attain true professional status, then effective staff development programs must play a vital role.

One final key reason for the new importance attached to staff development is the recent emphasis placed on accountability and the resultant need for school districts to produce evidence of effective teaching and learning. In their quest for academic excellence and higher levels of productivity as reflected in rising standardized test scores, school districts have come to realize that there is simply no substitute for a competent professional teacher in every classroom. Technology, supplies, materials, and equipment are only as good as the teachers who employ these resources to help students reach their academic and personal potential. The realization of this fundamental truth has been a driving force behind efforts to improve staff development programs for teachers.

Our purpose in this chapter is to explore the potential for using staff development as a tool for promoting growth and renewal of teachers at the school level. We believe it is important to focus our discussion at the school level because the evidence is overwhelming that individual schools hold the greatest potential for meaningful change. The school level is also the place where teacher leaders have the greatest opportunity to influence the design, organization, and implementation of growth activities that can make teaching more exciting, productive, and personally and professionally rewarding.

We begin our discussion of staff development with a brief overview of the characteristics and needs of adult learners, followed by an exploration of the career stages of teachers. A realization of the important differences in how adults and children learn, coupled with an understanding of how teachers develop over a career, leads us to a description of the characteristics and conditions for effective staff development programs. A detailed description of how teacher leaders can use what is known about effective staff development programs to design and implement successful programs in their own schools is the concluding section in this chapter.

Adults as Learners

One of the more enduring problems with staff development programs for teachers has been the propensity of staff developers to treat adult learners as children, rather than as adults. We already alluded to the high level of dissatisfaction that teachers traditionally have expressed with efforts directed toward their professional development. Being treated like children is, without question, one of the primary sources of their discontent.

The term *pedagogy*, which commonly has been equated with the art and science of teaching children, has, until quite recently, provided the structure for designing learning activities for adults as well. Pedagogy is essentially teacher centered in that the teacher determines what is to be learned, how it is to be learned, when it will be learned, and how what is learned will be measured. The learner is the passive receiver of the instruction and is dependent on the knowledge, skill, and most of all, direction of the teacher (Knowles, 1990). This teacher-centered approach to learning is not well suited to the needs of adults (Dalellew & Martinez, 1988; Merriam, 1993; Moore, 1988).

A theory of adult learning commonly referred to as *andragogy* (Knowles, 1980, 1984, 1990) has gained increased attention in the professional literature. Andragogy, which builds on research and practice from adult education and psychology, has served to provide a framework that those concerned with providing staff development opportunities may use in designing learning experiences for adults that more closely match their needs and preferences for learning. This task can be accomplished through gaining an understanding of the fundamental differences between adult learners and their younger counterparts and then adjusting for these differences in the design and implementation of learning experiences for adults. First, let's consider some of the more important differences.

Obviously, some important physical differences exist between older and younger learners, although some of these differences may not be as pronounced as previously thought (Merriam, 1993). As human beings mature, their bodies become less tolerant of environmental irregularities, and as a group they tend to function at a more subdued pace. We hasten to add, however, that adult learners do not necessarily have a diminished ability to learn. Adult learners generally can learn as well as, and in some respects better than, younger learners because of the quantity and variety of previous life experiences they have accumulated. As opposed to some other groups, adults generally are unwilling to sit and listen passively for extended periods of time. They prefer to be actively involved in learning tasks, giving and receiving feedback, testing ideas on others, and engaging in a broad range of activities.

Adult learners need to be more self-directing than young learners. As an individual matures, the natural inclination is to assume more responsibility for all aspects of one's life, to make choices based on personal preference and experience, and to take responsibility for those choices. Mature adults place a very high value on independence. When they find themselves in situations that stifle their need to be self-directing, they are likely to experience some anxiety and tension. In such situations, they can be expected to respond with expressions of resentment and even active resistance.

Adult learners tend to be present, rather than future, oriented. They seek to learn new skills and acquire knowledge that can be applied readily in the short term to help them cope successfully with real-life problems, tasks, and objectives. Mature learners choose to learn what they are convinced they need to learn, rather than to learn what someone else thinks they need to learn. Teachers, for example, want the demands of their particular work situations and the practical problems they face in the everyday world of work, as reflected in the classroom, to be the focus of their continuing professional education. As is true for most adult learners, teachers must be convinced that proposed new learning is readily applicable to their lives—that it is, in fact, essential to their present well-being—so that they personally may validate the value of the learning. Because of this need to validate the value of learning, adult learners tend to be intrinsically motivated to learn, whereas less mature learners are more prone to rely on extrinsic motivation to encourage them to put forth the necessary effort to learn.

The quantity and variety of previous experiences are a key difference between more and less mature learners. Adults expect that their knowledge and experience will be respected and that these attributes will form the bedrock of new learning experiences. Although experiences randomly happen to children, adults, as mature individuals, strive to shape their new experiences. In this way, adults hope to exert some control over their destinies. Most adults define who they are, not just by their past experiences, but by the independence and freedom they believe they can exercise to influence what happens around them. To comprehend this notion is to understand that to discount a person's experience is to devalue the person; to ignore that person's experience is closely akin to rejecting the person.

The experiences of adults are among the richest resources available for new learning. These experiences can be a mixed blessing, however, because bias and false operating assumptions are the frequent traveling companions of experience. So, although a person's experiences should always be respected, careful attention must be directed toward eliminating bias and correcting false assumptions so that more efficacious attitudes and opinions can assume their places and thus allow the person to grow to his or her maximum potential.

One final important consideration related to understanding differences between the learning needs of children and adults is the recognition that, as people grow and mature, they go through a series of life and career stages. Educators have long recognized the effects that a child's physical, emotional, and psychological states have on learning. Adults are similarly affected. It is just that adults are at different places in the continuum of life and career than children. Because an understanding of career stages is central to designing a staff development plan responsive to all teachers, we devote considerable space to this subject a little later in this chapter.

Pedagogy-andragogy represents a continuum ranging from teacher-directed to student-directed learning (Knowles, 1980). Both approaches are appropriate with children and adults, depending on the situation (Dalellew & Martinez, 1988; Merriam, 1993). For example, borrowing from pedagogy, adults who know little or nothing about a topic may benefit from teacher-directed instruction until they have sufficient knowledge to assume more responsibility for directing their own learning. Likewise, there are implications for pedagogy in many of the principles of andragogy: creation of a climate where learners feel respected, trusted, and cared about; establishment of the idea that a real need to know exists before instruction begins; and extension of freedom to learners to help select methods and resources for learning.

TABLE 7.1   Behaviors and Conditions That Facilitate Adult
Learning

Facilitative	*Nonfacilitative*
Informal tone	Formal tone
Nondirective	Directive
Open body language	Closed body language
Easy manner	Intimidating manner
Sensitivity to others	Insensitivity to others
Respecting experience	Discounting experience
Reciprocal trust	Suspicion
Thought-provoking questions	Narrow, factual questions
Soliciting answers	Giving answers
Providing choices	Never giving choices
Good listening skills	Poor listening skills
Encouraging interaction	Discouraging interaction

Andragogy does not totally define the uniqueness of adult learning, any more than pedagogy totally defines the uniqueness of children learning. Andragogy does, however, suggest a set of conditions for designing staff development programs for adult learners who have clearly identifiable needs, including the need to be more self-directed than teacher-directed. Table 7.1 lists behaviors and conditions that facilitate adult learning. Teacher leaders should do everything in their power to see that facilitative behaviors are practiced and facilitative conditions are fostered in all situations where adults are expected to profit from staff development opportunities.

Now that we have touched on the importance of understanding the special needs of adult learners in relation to providing them with professional growth experiences, we turn our attention to a discussion of the career stages of teachers. In our view, it is equally important to recognize the professional growth needs of teachers on the basis of their career stages as it is to understand the unique needs of adult learners as opposed to younger learners. After a discussion of the career stages of teachers, we summarize what we have learned about adult learners as it relates to the career stages of teachers in order to suggest a set of conditions that should guide the creation of staff development programs for teachers.

Career Stages of Teachers

It is widely recognized that teacher expertise is developed over an extended period of time (Berliner, 1994; Burke, Christenson, & Fessler, 1984; Glatthorn, 1994; Glickman, 1981). On the journey to achieving true professional status, teachers pass through a series of normal and predictable stages. Berliner (1994), for example, suggested that teachers move through five distinct stages: novice, advanced beginner, competent, proficient, and expert.

Every teacher must go through an induction period that is a transition from preservice teacher training to being a full-fledged member of the teaching force. These "greenhorns," whom Berliner labeled novice teachers, are typically student teachers or beginning teachers who are experiencing for the first time what Veenman (1984) termed the "reality shock" of managing their own classrooms. Even though teaching skills are taught during preservice, many beginning teachers believe that they never acquired them or that they were inadequately taught. In truth, prospective teachers do not even know the right questions to ask during their preservice training because they do not have the experiential framework that provides substance and context to real teaching problems. Because they lack this practical experience, novice teachers must devote an inordinate amount of their time and energy to gaining a working understanding of the classroom environment, mastering the basic tasks to be performed, and formulating a set of general rules to guide their daily actions in working with students. According to Berliner (1994), "The novice teacher is taught the meaning of terms like 'higher order questions,' 'reinforcement,' and 'learning disabled,' . . . and rules such as 'give praise for right answer,' 'wait three seconds after asking a higher order question,' and 'never criticize a student' " (p. 6021).

With a little experience, the novice becomes an advanced beginner. Advanced beginners tend to be in their second or third year of teaching and still feel many of the insecurities of novices.

However, they are beginning to build up "episodic" and "case" knowledge to help them deal with many problems commonly faced by teachers in the classroom. In many areas, advanced beginners are still unsure of how to react to specific problems when they arise and when to follow or break some of the rules of teaching they acquired during the novice stage. Berliner (1994) made the point that "context begins to guide behavior. . . . For example, teachers learn that praise does not always have the desired effect, as when a low-ability child interprets it as communicating low expectations" (p. 6021). As is also true for novices, advanced beginners often fail to take full responsibility for their actions in the classroom because they still are applying the rules of teaching in a rote, mechanical fashion without really recognizing what is happening.

With additional experience and hard work, most teachers reach the third stage of career development—the competent teacher. Berliner (1994) pointed out two distinguishing characteristics of competent performers. First, they make conscious choices about what they are going to do by setting priorities and developing plans based on rational goals and logical means for achieving those goals. Second, while executing their plans, they know what is important and what is not, what to ignore and what to pay attention to. In so doing, they avoid many "timing" and "targeting" errors. In short, competent teachers are generally in control of their classrooms and practice their teaching skills in context. This control leads them to recognize and accept responsibility for successes and failures because they are not so detached from teaching as are novices and advanced beginners.

Sometime around the fifth year of teaching, Berliner (1994) asserted, a "modest" number of teachers reach the proficient stage. This stage is characterized by "intuition" or "know-how." Proficient teachers acquire a "holistic" sense of what is occurring in the classroom and can recognize similarities and differences among events that occur in the classroom and respond accordingly. Berliner likened reaching this stage with finally overcoming the problems associated with learning how to dance. Whereas a novice dancer may expend considerable effort just watching his or her feet and counting the steps, a proficient dancer is free to forget about the basics and just move with the music. The freedom, the smooth masterful flow that can come only with the ability to recognize and understand the multitude of repeating patterns that are at the heart of the teaching act (or dancing act), distinguishes the proficient teacher (or dancer) from teachers (or dancers) at earlier stages of development.

"If the novice is deliberate, the advanced beginner insightful, the competent performer rational, and the proficient performer intuitive, the expert might be categorized as often arational" (Berliner, 1994, p. 6022). Although it seems strange to characterize a person who is expert at something as arational, Berliner had good reason for choosing this term. Expert teachers perform their work in a way that is "qualitatively" different from others. They have the innate ability to sense the appropriate response to every situation and are seemingly able to do this without having to analyze situations or even to make conscious choices about what to do. Expert teachers are so inherently skilled that lessons under their direction seem to move along effortlessly. Expert teachers may not even appear to be central to what is happening in the classroom, much as expert basketball officials are able to officiate games without drawing undue attention to themselves.

Like theories of adult learning, theories of the developmental stages of teaching have heuristic value for thinking about staff development opportunities for teachers. Understanding that all teachers pass through readily identifiable developmental stages can help teacher leaders realize that teachers at different stages have different needs, as well as different capabilities to benefit from a range of staff development activities. For example, during the early stages of development, teachers are self-centered out of necessity. Novice or advanced beginners may naturally be more concerned with their own survival in the classroom than they are with how much children are learning. Their unique staff development interests may be served best by programs that focus on arming them with survival skills, such as workshops dealing with organization and management of the classroom. When they are in the middle stages of development, teachers are beginning to master their craft and to gain control of their surroundings. At this point in their development, they are capable of shifting their focus away from personal survival needs to the needs of their students. They can be expected to focus their attention on practicing and refining their skills and techniques. Unlike novices, teachers at the middle development levels would have little need for staff development activities designed to build skills in classroom management but might be eager to learn new experimental strategies designed to raise student performance.

At the highest levels of development, teachers become much more integrated personalities with the capabilities and resources to provide leadership that extends beyond themselves and their students. Although the perceived need for inservice training on the part of expert teachers may be expected to decline with increasing years of experience (Meinick, 1989), it may very well be a time for them to share their talents and abilities on a broader basis with others in their schools, their districts, and the profession at large.

Preservice teacher education is charged with the responsibility of preparing prospective teachers to enter the initial, or novice, stage of teacher development. However, succeeding career stages must be achieved while teachers are on the job, either through experience in the classroom or participation in staff development activities. This knowledge should serve to underscore the importance of staff development to the well-being of millions of individual teachers and, consequently, to the profession as well. It should be the aim of every staff development program to help every teacher progress as far as possible along the continuum of professional development. The following section discusses some of the more important conditions for building effective staff development programs. This is followed by a step-by-step description of a process to design, implement, and evaluate a staff development program at the school level.

Necessary Conditions for Effective
Staff Development for Teachers

The foregoing discussion painted in rather broad brush strokes a picture of the unique professional growth needs of teachers, who have been characterized as adult learners passing through a series of stages of career development. If teacher leaders are to use this information wisely, they must translate it into a series of guidelines or conditions that will help shape the design and implementation of successful staff development programs for teachers. With this in mind, we believe that the following conditions are critical to the development of such programs.

1. *The teacher must be at the absolute center of the staff development process.* Individual teachers and groups of teachers must assume the primary responsibility for their own professional growth. Relying on others to determine their needs and how those needs can best be met has not worked in the past and will not work in the future. Teachers must be given the freedom and responsibility for planning staff development in terms of diagnosing their own learning needs, prioritizing those needs, designing and identifying programs and resources to meet the identified needs, and deciding when the needs have been adequately met. Placing teachers at the center of the staff development process means they not only will determine the nature and scope of programs for their own professional growth but also will assume a major share of the responsibility for helping and supporting each other in their efforts to grow.

2. *Staff development programs for teachers must be characterized by a climate of mutual professional respect.* Professional growth is greatly enhanced when teachers acknowledge and respect the professional talents and abilities of their colleagues. This is the critical ingredient that allows teachers to teach and learn from each other. Mutual professional respect prohibits competitiveness, encourages support, and ensures that the knowledge, skills and abilities of all teacher involved in professional development are recognized and celebrated.

3. *Learning must be related directly to the needs and interests of the adult learner participants in staff development programs.* Adequate provision must be made for participants to give and receive feedback in relation to the relevance of the programs in which they are engaged. Furthermore, participants should be helped and encour-

aged to apply the concepts, theories, and principles learned while participating in staff development activities to everyday situations confronted in their schools and in their classrooms.

4. *Professional growth experiences for teachers must make allowances for special consideration of the adult learner's unique mental, physical, and emotional needs.* Self-determination should be at the center of any professional growth plan for teachers. In the light of the vast differences in career and life stages of teachers, staff development activities should be characterized by a wide variety of growth experiences, freedom for participants to design for themselves or choose those experiences that best serve individual needs, and a climate that not only allows but also encourages risk taking and experimentation.

5. *The primary focus of staff development programs for teachers should be on sustained long-term growth.* It is quite clear that one-shot quick-fix approaches to staff development have little to offer teachers in terms of real professional growth. The reason one-shot staff development has not been more growth enhancing for teachers is that instruction typically is delivered at the lower levels (knowledge and comprehension) of the cognitive domain. Teachers, therefore, are not afforded needed opportunities to apply and practice new skills (application), much less to adapt them to their present teaching repertoires (synthesis) or to make judgments about how well they are working (evaluation) and then determine the reasons why they work or do not work (analysis). This approach to staff development overemphasizes narrowly defined, technical teaching models that trivialize the complexities of teaching and encourage teachers to function as technicians rather than as professionals. Only when teachers are encouraged to function at the higher levels of the cognitive domain can real growth be expected. Experience has taught us that successful implementation and maintenance do not necessarily follow successful initial training. The implementation of skills and strategies foreign to a teacher's existing repertoire requires more substantial training than typically has been provided (Gingiss, 1992). Teacher leaders must concern themselves with helping teachers experience

real professional growth, rather than with futilely trying to fix what is wrong with them. This task can best be achieved over extended periods that allow teachers to move beyond the lower levels of cognitive thinking.

6. *The focus for staff development programs needs to shift from inservice to what has been termed "onservice"* (Gardner, 1994). Teacher leaders can facilitate the impact of onservice by developing "in-house experts" on topics the faculty identifies as important (e.g., cooperative learning, global education, values education, inclusive education). Volunteers who would like to become in-house experts can be sent to key workshops and "training of trainers" conferences. They then will be resident experts on staff, available for training their fellow teachers and troubleshooting for them as they attempt to implement innovations selected by the faculty. Several powerful advantages are associated with onservice. Teachers are not removed from schools and, as such, are encouraged to focus on the realities of their own schools and classrooms. Onservice relies less on outside resources and expertise, promoting instead mutual respect and support of teachers for the skills and talents of their fellow teachers. And, as we pointed out earlier, the school is the primary unit of meaningful educational change. When the school becomes the focal point for most staff development, there is increased potential to build consensus and develop a true team spirit that simply cannot be achieved in other ways.

We believe that the six conditions outlined above are the most important guidelines to follow when designing and implementing staff development programs for teachers. The reader probably has noticed that what we proposed is not particularly detailed or comprehensive. We did not say what specific content should be included in staff development programs for teachers or how research should be factored in or even how programs should be conducted. We did not mention any of these things because we are much more concerned with the nature of the programs than we are with the detailed substance. In our opinion, the specific whats, wheres, whens, hows, and whos of staff development should be the domain of teachers, not the writers of books and articles. All educators must learn to trust and respect the professionalism and resourcefulness of teachers working individually and in groups to accomplish what they need to accomplish. After all, isn't this the very essence of teacher leadership?

In the section to follow, we briefly outline the steps required to design and implement a staff development program at the school level. It is our intention that teacher leaders will adapt this general outline to the specific situations in which they may be working.

Planning and Implementing
a School-Level Staff Development Program

We have already made it clear that the majority of staff development should occur at the school level. This is not to say that no activities can or should be organized at the district or even multi-district levels. However, activities away from the school should not drive the staff development program. The needs of individual schools and the teachers and other staff members within those schools should be at the forefront of staff development efforts. With this in mind, the majority of the resources for staff development should be allocated directly to schools. If this is not currently the practice in your school district, then the teachers, administrators, and other staff members should work in concert to see that increased resources are provided to the schools. Staff development should be a total school activity. Although a small team of teachers and other staff members may be used to coordinate the process, every member of the faculty should be involved in helping to plan and implement the school's staff development program. Many roles are available—for example, assisting with the task of assessing and prioritizing staff development needs, making needed logistical arrangements for training to take place, presenting sessions for colleagues, and teaming with others in peer coaching or mentoring relationships. The overall success of the staff development program will depend, in large measure, on the level of involvement of the faculty and staff.

We believe that a staff development coordinating committee should be established in each school to provide direction to the staff development program. This committee should be small enough to function well in meetings, but at the same time be representative of the various grade levels, subjects, special programs, and services offered in the school. Although we recognize that the staff of a school should decide who will serve on such a committee, we recommend that the committee be both diverse and inclusive, as illustrated by a committee that includes a teacher from each grade level or subject area, a special education teacher, a counselor, a media specialist, and a member of the administrative team. Some schools even include a representative from each of the major support services in the school (e.g., clerical, housekeeping/ maintenance, and food service) on the staff development coordinating committee.

Figure 7.1 depicts a set of steps that can be used in planning, designing, and implementing a staff development program. Although most people generally think of planning as occurring near the beginning of a complex process, planning should be an ongoing activity throughout the entire staff development process. Planning is needed for conducting a needs assessment to start the process. However, planning is just as important to ensure the success of each remaining stage of the process.

Assessing and Prioritizing Needs

Conducting a needs assessment and prioritizing the needs may be the most critical step in the staff development process. If this activity is done poorly or not at all (as happens in some places), then the rest of the process will be invalid. Needs should not be determined from any one data source but should be a pulling together of multiple data sources to get the best overall picture of what is needed to promote the maximum opportunities for growth for all of those in the school. Some of the sources to be considered are school philosophy and goals; school performance reports, including such things as school improvement plans, test scores, dropout studies, student follow-up studies, and accreditation reports; faculty and staff surveys; committee, grade-level, and

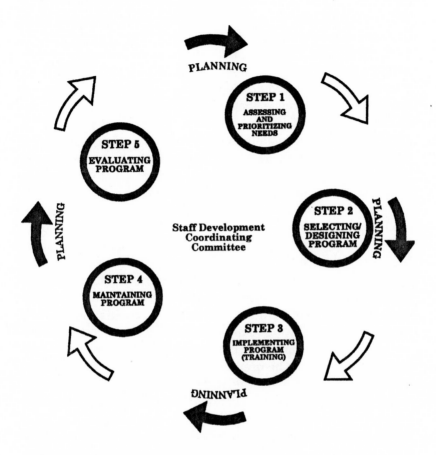

Figure 7.1. Staff Development Process

department meetings; and individual professional improvement goals.

Many school districts take a rather informal approach to staff development needs assessment. It has long been a common practice for someone at the district level to draft a memorandum in the early spring to survey potential program participants about their staff development needs. The substance of the memorandum generally consists of a statement that plans are being made for staff development for the coming school year and a request for recipients of the memorandum to list, in the space provided, their preferences for topics to be included in the inservice program and to return it to the district office. Someone at the district office then reviews the returned forms and compiles a list of the most requested topics. These topics, which are often more of the same old thing (e.g., classroom management, motivating students), once again form the backbone of the staff development program for another year. Unfortunately, in many locations, what we have just described is the extent of teacher involvement in planning for staff development. The only real planning teachers get to do is to plan to attend the sessions when they are offered!

If staff development is to be truly responsive to the needs of teachers and students, then assessment should be conducted on three levels within a school. Conducting a needs assessment at the first level—the school level—is the responsibility of the staff development coordinating committee. Data sources with schoolwide impact, such as school performance reports, school improvement plans, student achievement results, and accreditation reports, should be studied by the committee to determine areas for schoolwide staff development needs. A series of discussions around these documents can be used to generate a list of possible topics for schoolwide staff development. For example, if an accreditation study indicates that a weak relationship exists between the school and the community it serves, then this finding might suggest a need for some staff development in the area of school-community relationships. Or, if one of the recommendations listed in a school performance report is that the school should focus more on the use of technology as a teaching tool, then this recommendation might suggest another area for staff development. Using data sources such as those suggested, the coordinating committee can generate a list of possible topics for staff development. These then can be shared with the remainder of the staff at a faculty meeting, and a general consensus may be reached regarding which areas will be pursued during the next staff development cycle. Or, after a meeting to discuss the committee's interpretation of the needs for schoolwide staff development, a survey can be prepared and sent to each of the staff members, asking them to respond as to their perceived need for inservice in each of the areas identified. Priorities for schoolwide staff development then can be determined through an analysis of the completed surveys.

A second level of needs assessment can take place among smaller groups of teachers with common teaching interests. For example, teachers may meet in teams by grade levels or by subject areas to discuss unique needs they may share for professional growth experiences. Using this approach, a group of mathematics teachers, for example, may decide that they would welcome some staff development aimed at planning and conducting math lab activities or in techniques for teaching the metric system. A group of special education teachers might express a need for some help with parent training and involvement. A group of fourth-grade teachers could decide that they would like staff development aimed at effective techniques for teaching creative writing.

The third level of needs assessment occurs with individual staff members. As is true with students, "adults in schools have a diversity of needs, interests and learning styles" (National Association of Secondary School Principals [NASSP], 1991, p. 1). Differences among teachers in terms of their needs for staff development are related to a host of factors, including the courses they teach, the students they serve, individual learning styles, differences in career stages, and personal interests. Districtwide or even schoolwide staff development is likely to miss the mark for a significant portion of any staff. Therefore, each staff member should be encouraged to set individual growth goals and to design plans to achieve those goals. The following are questions that individuals might use to conduct a personal assessment of staff development needs and to establish a plan to meet those needs.

1. What are my strengths as a professional teacher?
2. What are some areas in which I might grow as a professional teacher?
3. What objectives can I establish to build on my strengths and improve areas that I perceive to be less strong?
4. What specific activities can I engage in to reach my objectives?
5. How will I know when I have achieved my objectives?

An unfortunate yet enduring fact of life is that there will generally always be more needs than there are resources to reach those needs. This is particularly true in the area of staff development. Therefore, the most important needs should be identified and served first. The most important needs can be determined by group consensus or even surveys. These techniques also seem to be quite effective in working with smaller groups of teachers, such as academic departments or grade-level teams. Figure 7.2 provides an example of a comprehensive staff development survey form that could be used with math teachers in a school. Part 1 of the form is designed to determine the priorities for schoolwide staff development; Part 2 examines priorities related specifically to the area of math; Part 3 seeks to gather information about teacher preferences for when and where staff development training should be delivered.

Selecting/Designing Programs

Based on the results of the assessment and prioritization of staff development needs, programs must be selected or designed to address those needs. Each individual component in a school's staff development plan should include the stated need to be addressed; the target audience; clear, measurable objectives; the approach that will be used to reach the objectives; time requirements; financial, as well as other resource requirements; and the method of evaluation. In our view, this is the minimum information needed to ensure that staff development activities will be well planned and effectively implemented.

We strongly suggest that traditional staff development workshops at which a presenter stands in front of a group and delivers a lecture be held to a minimum. There are so many preferable alternatives to this approach that it should be used only when the objectives (e.g., creating a level of awareness) dictate that a group presentation is the most effective and efficient way to go. In fact, the trend in staff development has many schools and teachers moving away from group workshops and toward collaborative arrangements that give teachers, administrators, university-based

Directions: For Items 1-10, circle the number that best reflects your level of need for staff development in each particular area. For Items 11-15, list other areas in which you think staff development is needed. For Items 16-20, indicate your preference for when staff development should take place.

Area	Levels of Need for Inservice Training			
	Great 1	Moderate 2	Some 3	None 4
Part One: All teachers				
1. Identifying needs and planning for individual differences among students	1	2	3	4
2. Using performance portfolios to measure student progress	1	2	3	4
3. Conducting classroom discussion/using questioning techniques	1	2	3	4
4. Using standardized tests and interpreting test data	1	2	3	4
5. Developing student self-concepts, attitudes, and values	1	2	3	4
Part Two: Mathematics teachers				
6. Planning and conducting math lab activities	1	2	3	4
7. Developing and using learning activity packets	1	2	3	4
8. Teaching the metric system	1	2	3	4
9. Relating math to real-life situations	1	2	3	4
10. Interpreting and using standardized test results	1	2	3	4
11. _____				
12. _____				
13. _____				
14. _____				
15. _____				
Part Three: All teachers				
	Staff Development Time Preferences			
	Highly Desirable 1	Somewhat Desirable 2	Undesirable 3	Highly Undesirable 4
16. Before-/after-school workshops at your school	1	2	3	4
17. Saturday workshops	1	2	3	4
18. Inservice day workshops	1	2	3	4
19. On-site workshops (during school day)	1	2	3	4
20. Summer workshops	1	2	3	4

Figure 7.2. Sample Needs Assessment Instrument

personnel, and others opportunities to work together in a variety of configurations.

One need not look far for examples of successful collaborations. The professional development schools movement that pairs universities with schools has spread rapidly across the country (Colburn, 1993). Professional development schools seek to improve instruction at the school level while enhancing teacher training at the university level. A good example of multilevel collaboration is the Mastery in Learning Project, sponsored by the National Education Association (NEA). The NEA established a network of 26 schools across the nation, committed to developing the capacity for continuous, comprehensive growth and change (NASSP, 1991). A computer-conferencing system affords practitioners in the member schools the opportunity to dialogue with researchers on a regular basis. The Essential Schools movement is yet another example of broadscale collaboration to improve teaching and learning in schools through promoting professional growth of teachers and administrators (Muncey & McQuillan, 1993; Sizer, 1988).

On the individual school level, a number of very effective collaborative approaches to promoting professional growth are available. Professional dialogue, an arrangement in which teachers meet at regularly scheduled times to discuss teaching, is being used in many schools across the country. The emphasis in professional dialogue is on developing reflective thinking that allows teachers to discuss and analyze together what they are doing in their individual classrooms. Sometimes the dialogue may be in response to a book or an article that the members of the group have read together. But always, the emphasis is on reflective thinking about teaching and learning. This technique is diametrically opposed to the emphasis on skill building, which is the substance of most traditional workshops.

Action research is another collaborative staff development tool that is becoming quite popular with teachers. With this approach, teachers identify a problem they are dealing with in the school. The problem is analyzed through the collection of data. Possible solutions are proposed and ultimately tested and evaluated in the classroom. For obvious reasons, this is a very exciting approach to professional development.

Peer coaching and mentoring have achieved tremendous popularity with teachers and administrators during the last 10 years. *Peer coaching* is the term used to describe a collegial relationship between teams of teachers who observe in the classroom and give feedback to one another on various aspects of their teaching effectiveness. *Mentoring* generally is used to denote a professional relationship in which a more experienced teacher assumes responsibility for assisting a less experienced teacher in making the transition from preservice teacher training to actual teaching. We believe that peer coaching and mentoring are so important to professional development that we have devoted the entire next chapter to a discussion of how they can be used most effectively in schools.

In addition to workshops and collaborative arrangements, individuals may design their own personal growth plans based on their own particular preferences and needs. Individual teachers can read books and articles, enroll in university courses, take trips, hold consultations with experts, or engage in any one of a number of activities to meet their professional and personal growth needs. The sky is the limit! Teacher leaders are constrained only by their imaginations and creative instincts when selecting and designing exciting and rewarding ways to promote the growth of teachers.

Implementing the Program

Plans must be implemented if they are to be useful. Responsibility for implementation should be shared. The staff development coordinating committee normally assumes responsibility for coordinating the implementation of schoolwide staff development activities. The committee meets on a monthly basis to oversee the implementation of the total program. Those activities that involve small groups of teachers, such as professional dialogue, and those that involve individual teachers generally are managed at the level at which they occur, although the coordinating committee still may maintain some budget oversight.

Implementation of a schoolwide staff development activity involves bringing together the trainer and those participating in the staff development activity at a particular time, in a particular location, with the necessary supplies, equipment, and materials required to carry out the established plan. Planning for each program must begin well in advance.

Three months before the proposed activity, the following tasks should have been completed: the content and format of the activity determined, a site selected and confirmed, and a presenter or presenters identified and confirmed. Eight weeks before the activity, the planning committee should confirm the room and seating arrangements and determine what equipment, supplies, and materials are needed at the staff development site. If the activity is not being held at the school, rental fees, dining arrangements, and accommodations for parking need to be determined. Concurrently, those who will be presenting need to receive information on the arrangements to accommodate the staff development activity. Arrangements for any special needs of the presenter(s), such as the duplication of materials, should be finalized at this time, together with travel plans, subsistence, and honoraria. All of these arrangements should be confirmed in writing with the presenter(s).

Five weeks before the planned activity, financial arrangements, such as the preparation of purchase requests for consultant services, facilities, materials, and supplies, should be finalized. Program bulletins or announcements should be prepared and distributed. Finally, 1 to 3 days before the activity is to take place, all arrangements should be checked to make sure everything is ready and in place.

When choosing presenters, we think it is best to look at home first. By using presenters from the coordinating committee's own school family, the committee is in a position to provide recognition to teacher leaders who already enjoy a high level of credibility and respect among their peers. The committee also is reinforcing the notion that human resources in the school are adequate to deal with the majority of the problems that concern teachers on a day-to-day basis. So, before the committee members look outside for staff development leadership, they should ask themselves these questions: Does someone on our staff have the expertise and skills to deliver the program? Does the person use effective group presentation techniques? Does he or she understand the objectives of the program, and can he or she deliver the program in a way that will meet the needs of adult learners? We believe that the answer to these questions is frequently a resounding Yes!

Maintaining the Program

Maintaining the program rests primarily with the staff development coordinating committee, but all teacher leaders must claim responsibility in this regard. Most unsuccessful school-based staff development programs fail, not because they are poorly executed, but because they lack the commitment, drive, and determination required to see good ideas through to a satisfactory conclusion. This is the identical problem plaguing the one-shot staff development workshop. Teachers attend a workshop, get excited about some of the new possibilities they are exposed to, and then gradually grow discouraged as the reality of dealing with students in the classroom chips away at their enthusiasm day by day.

Genuine change is a slow and difficult process. Most people tend to oppose radical alterations in what is currently happening around them even when the proposed changes appear to be desirable. The amount of change required not only affects teachers' willingness to try something new but also has a bearing on their ability to sustain the changes over a period of time. Therefore, it is generally best to begin with modest changes that will result in positive student gains in a relatively short time. Practices that are new and unfamiliar will be abandoned unless evidence of their positive effects can be seen. Depending on the complexity of the change, it may take as long as 5 years to see significant improvement. And nearly always, an "implementation dip" will occur as things get worse before they get better. During this difficult time, attempts at change are most likely to be abandoned. When teachers see that a new program or innovation enhances the learning outcomes of their students, then and only then will significant changes be made in their beliefs and attitudes (Guskey, 1985b).

The considerable effort required to make positive changes over a period of time requires a viable support system for teachers. Teachers need regular and specific feedback on their efforts and the resultant student outcomes. Continued support and follow-up are extremely critical after initial training. Both time and experimentation are required to adapt new approaches to individual classrooms while still maintaining program fidelity. During these periods of growth and development, teachers need to know that help and support are readily available. That is the goal of maintenance in the staff development process. In the next chapter, we discuss in detail how peer coaching can be used as an effective tool to help sustain growth through periods of change brought about through staff development.

Evaluating the Program

The use of formative and summative evaluation for each activity included in the school's staff development plan is critical to improving the program in future years. It may not be reasonable to expect that significant change in teachers' attitudes and practices can be assessed effectively at the end of any training session, no matter how intense. Significant change requires time and practice. In fact, several years of practice and feedback may be required before individual participants achieve the objectives of training.

The most important consideration may be to structure the evaluation prior to training so that the results can be keyed to improving staff development, rather than for political or other purposes. Here are some questions to help guide evaluation:

1. What is the purpose of the evaluation?
2. Will the focus of evaluation be on long-range outcomes, short-range outcomes, or both?
3. How will outcomes be determined?
4. How will the evaluation results be used? To improve the plan? To seek support for additional resources? To measure the efficacy of the plan?

If questions like these are answered prior to evaluation, then the results are likely to justify the investment of time and energy required to carry out the evaluation plan.

A Final Word About Staff Development

There can be little doubt that the greatest potential for improving professional performance in our nation's schools over the long haul is locked in staff development efforts at the school level. Furthermore, it is becoming quite clear that teacher leadership for improving staff development is the key to unlocking that potential and to releasing a tremendous wave of creativity and energy spawned by tens of thousands of teachers in classrooms across the country.

Staff development offers many worthwhile benefits to teachers. It can effectively provide the keys to improving professional performance, reducing isolation, providing a support system, and generally improving the professional lives of teachers by making them more pleasurable and productive. When teacher leaders accept the responsibility to plan and implement the staff development efforts at their schools, they accept a tremendous challenge. That challenge is to make staff development so exciting, so effective, so worthwhile, and so clearly attuned to the growth needs of their colleagues that every single one of them will demand to be a part of the program.

8

Peer Coaching

Teachers Helping Teachers
One-on-One

Introduction

Imagine for a moment the following exchange occurring between two teaching colleagues:

Linda: Susan, that was really fun watching you teach that lesson today!

Susan: I'm glad you had fun. But I have to admit I'm still a little nervous having another adult in my classroom, even though I know you aren't there to evaluate me.

Linda: Yes, I know what you mean by nervous. But isn't it a wonderful feeling to be able to share what we do with another adult who genuinely cares? I have learned so much from watching you teach, having you watch me, and sharing ideas about how to do the job better. I really look forward to the time we spend together discussing our observations.

I don't know about you, Susan, but for the first time in a long while I'm excited about teaching my students. I feel as if I'm a better teacher now than I've ever been before. And you know what? I think that with your help and support, I'm going to be even better.

Susan: Gosh, Linda, you make me feel simply wonderful! How in the world did we survive before we got into this peer coaching thing?

Does this conversation sound foreign to you? Unfortunately, it sounds as if it comes straight out of a fantasyland to many of this nation's teachers. But more and more, similar conversations are taking place in schools all across the country as teachers become involved in a variety of collegial relationships designed to help each other grow as professional teachers.

Teachers working together in collegial relationships to help one another improve instructional effectiveness is not a new phenomenon. In fact, programs designed for this purpose have existed in isolation for more than 35 years (Glatthorn, 1984). However, collaborative working relationships among teachers for the purpose of improving instruction are increasingly being used by school districts to supplement or replace the one-shot workshops that have proven so ineffective in promoting the professional growth of teachers in the past (Ackland, 1991). The rapid development and expansion of such programs is one of the most exciting and significant breakthroughs in both teacher leadership and professional growth for teachers to come about in a very long time.

Various terms have been used in the literature to describe a variety of collaborative working arrangements among teachers to improve instructional effectiveness. *Cooperative professional development, peer supervision, collegial supervision, peer review, team coaching, mentoring, peer observation, cognitive coaching,* and *peer coaching* have all been used to describe such arrangements (Ackland, 1991; Glatthorn, 1984; Joyce & Showers, 1982; Mohlman, Kierstead, & Gundlach, 1982; Sparks, 1990).

Although some subtle and other not so subtle differences exist among the approaches labeled by the variety of titles mentioned above, we have chosen the term *peer coaching* for use throughout the remainder of this chapter to describe the process whereby teams of teachers regularly observe one another teaching and provide support and feedback to promote mutual growth for all concerned. We have chosen *peer coaching* as a representative term for two reasons: (a) It seems to be the most common term used in the literature to describe teacher-to-teacher techniques for promoting professional development, and (b) the term seems to capture the essence of this special relationship between teachers in that it speaks directly to equality.

The purpose of this chapter is to present and discuss peer coaching by addressing the following questions:

- What is the nature of peer coaching?
- What is peer coaching, and what sets it apart from other, more traditional methods of working with teachers to improve instruction?
- How can a teacher leader use peer coaching to assist colleagues in becoming more effective in the classroom?
- How can a peer coaching program be established in a school?

The Nature of Peer Coaching

Peer coaching is an approach that encourages teachers to work with other teachers in an open, collegial relationship by using a process for addressing instructional improvement based on data gathered from classroom observations. Peer coaching is based on the belief that lasting improvement in teacher performance most likely will result from the careful use of a systematic process practiced jointly by teachers in a supportive and nonjudgmental relationship. This unique integration of interpersonal awareness and systematic method marks peer coaches as educators who are both caring and technically competent.

Table 8.1 presents a summary of some of the more important differences between peer coaching and other more traditional approaches to working with teachers in supervisory arrangements.

TABLE 8.1 Peer Coaching Versus Traditional Supervision

Peer Coaching	Traditional Supervision
Voluntary	Mandatory
Collegial	Hierarchical
Teacher directed	Other directed
Highly structured	Largely unstructured
Nonjudgmental	Highly judgmental
Time-consuming	Time efficient
Concentrated focus	Global focus
Nonevaluative	Evaluative
Promotes teacher growth	Fosters teacher dependence

Although any one of these differences in isolation is significant, taken together they represent widely divergent approaches to working with teachers to bring about instructional improvement.

Peer coaching is voluntary in two respects: (a) Teachers volunteer to take part in peer coaching, and (b) they also volunteer to work with colleagues of their choosing (Desrochers & Klein, 1990; Glatthorn, 1984; Phillips & Glickman, 1991). This approach is directly opposed to a more traditional approach to supervision in which teachers are required to take part in supervisory activities on a mandated schedule at the direction of someone else in the school organization, such as the principal or a district-level supervisor. Typically, teachers who are subjected to traditional supervisory practices have no choice about whom they will work with during the supervision process.

Peer coaching is characterized by a highly collegial relationship among a small group of teachers (generally two or three). This relationship is based on mutual respect for each other's abilities, a willingness to accept each other as a source of help and support, and a realization that all are working toward a common goal: to improve the quality of the instruction available to students. Traditionally, teachers have been supervised by someone who is perceived to be superior (e.g., principal) in the educational hierarchy. This option has left little room for a mutual exploration of ideas and approaches because it generally has been assumed that the superior will take the lead in both identifying the problems to be solved and providing the solutions.

Unlike more traditional approaches to supervision, peer coaching is intended to be teacher directed. Although administrators frequently are involved in assisting with the establishment of peer coaching programs, the recommended approach is that teachers ultimately assume responsibility for coordinating and directing such programs (Desrochers & Klein, 1990; Glatthorn, 1984). Important decisions related to peer coaching should be made by teachers, rather than by administrators or supervisors.

Although there are numerous peer coaching models with varying stages or steps, almost all of the models share three common elements: (a) a preobservation conference, (b) an observation, and (c) a postobservation conference (Desrochers & Klein, 1990; Glatthorn, 1984; Mohlman et al., 1982). Many readers will recognize that the three common elements of the peer coaching process are also at the heart of the clinical supervision process (Cogan, 1973; Goldhammer, 1969). What makes peer supervision unique, however, is not the three common elements that are shared with clinical supervision, but how and by whom they are practiced. Traditional supervision may or may not include the three common elements shared by clinical and peer supervision. In reality, there is no single recognized model of traditional supervision. The truth is that there are as many versions of traditional supervision as there are those who practice it.

Peer supervision encourages teachers to become more introspective about their teaching through techniques that cause them to think about the results of their teaching behaviors in the classroom. These techniques include asking questions carefully designed to help teachers assess their teaching situation for themselves; providing wait time to improve the quality of students' thinking; probing for specificity, clarity, and precision; listening carefully; and paraphrasing. The peer coach is also very careful to respond in a nonjudgmental manner to everything the teacher says or does. This approach is directly opposed to more traditional approaches to supervision in which supervisors frequently are perceived as being highly judgmental and directive in their dealings with teachers.

Peer coaching requires considerably more time than other, more traditional approaches to supervision. This is the result of the structured nature of the peer supervision process, coupled with the indirect approach used in identifying and solving problems. It should be noted, however, that the time invested in the peer coaching process is much more likely to produce significant and lasting results in terms of teacher improvement.

Peer coaching employs a concentrated focus to instructional improvement, as opposed to the more global approaches frequently featured by traditional supervision. During a peer coaching cycle, the teacher and the coach usually focus on one or two specific teaching behaviors in the classroom, such as verbal and/or nonverbal reinforcement of student participation. The areas to receive emphasis are predetermined by the teacher being observed, in consultation with the coach. Other aspects of teaching, such as classroom management, structure of the lesson, and use of higher order questions, are ignored in favor of focusing attention on the areas agreed on. Traditional approaches to supervision are typically very global in this respect and include all aspects of teaching with no particular focus. In fact, traditional supervisors frequently rely on generic checklists with a broad range of teaching behaviors to be observed.

The peer coaching process is nonevaluative. Data collected and shared during the peer coaching process are as objective and specific as possible, to the extent that they can be placed in a category or categories (higher order questions vs. lower order questions) and/or quantified (1 higher order question asked, 21 lower order questions asked). This approach is opposed to more traditional approaches to supervision in which value judgments are attached to what happens in the classroom and opinions tend to predominate (e.g., The teacher asked too many questions during the lesson).

Peer coaching is confidential and is never used for purposes of evaluation; rather, it is intended to foster mutual growth on the part of the participants. Traditional supervision, although purporting to foster the improvement of instruction, frequently has as a second purpose the attachment of a summative evaluation.

The results of peer coaching support long-term teacher growth and teacher independence. This is so because the peer coaching process makes teachers full and equal partners in helping to identify and solve instructional problems for themselves, as well as for others. Rather than provide teachers with narrow solutions to idiosyncratic problems, as is frequently true in traditional approaches to supervision, peer coaching allows teachers to practice a structured approach to problem solving that encourages them to become more insightful and introspective in dealing with a broad range of teaching problems. This approach is what makes peer coaching truly helpful; the job of teaching is performed better than it was before peer coaching occurred, and all participants in the peer coaching process become more independent and better able to solve their own problems in the future as a result of taking part in peer coaching.

Assumptions Undergirding Peer Supervision

Peer coaching is far more than a process illustrated by a series of stages. In a larger sense, it is an attitude that reflects one's acceptance of several basic assumptions. Reaching a comfort level with these assumptions is necessary in order to promote a collegial working relationship among teachers that ultimately results in improved instruction and better learning conditions for children.

Research has demonstrated that, on the whole, teachers are very dissatisfied with supervision as it has been practiced traditionally and generally hold supervisors in low regard. Evidence is also ample that teachers do not think supervision helps them improve their instructional effectiveness. Peer coaching is designed to circumvent some of the shortcomings of traditional supervision by changing the nature of the working relationship among teachers who are striving to improve instruction. This change can best be accomplished when teacher leaders are willing to embrace the following set of assumptions:

Assumption 1:   The fundamental purpose of peer coaching is to improve instruction by encouraging teachers to work together as colleagues.

If peer coaching is to be effective, then teachers must see each other as helpers, not as evaluators. If peer coaches are perceived as wearing two hats—the helper hat and the evaluator hat—the resulting role ambiguity is sure to prevent them from performing either function well. If teachers perceive that the focus of a peer coach is something other than the improvement of instruction, then they will be less likely to reveal themselves in a professional sense, and it becomes highly unlikely that meaningful growth will take place.

Clearly, most people learn best in a threat-free environment that fosters mutual support, respect, and collegiality. By focusing on a person's strengths, rather than weaknesses, and by avoiding being placed in situations that force them to be judgmental, peer coaches can establish the kind of professional climate that promotes optimal growth. For this reason, when serving as peer coaches, teacher leaders must vigorously resist pressures that may be exerted on them by principals and others to assume the role of evaluator.

Assumption 2: Many instructional problems encountered by the teacher in the classroom can be resolved if the teacher changes his or her behavior in positive ways.

Many things affect a student's thoughts and actions in a classroom—for example, his or her home environment, peer pressure, previous educational experiences, and mental and physical characteristics. Teachers have very little control over these things. However, teachers do have control over their own behavior. Teaching can be thought of as a series of patterns. The teacher produces an action, the student reacts, the teacher responds to the student, who in turn responds to the teacher, and so on. By changing the ways in which they interact with students, teachers can overcome many teaching difficulties. A teacher's own behavior is the one classroom factor over which the teacher has total control. Peer coaches can, in effect, serve as a mirror to help their fellow teachers see and understand their teaching behaviors and how these behaviors affect students.

Assumption 3: A firm bond of trust must be established between peer coaches if meaningful improvement is to take place.

The ability to create and maintain a trusting relationship is critical to the success of peer coaching. The peer coaching process is designed to identify and focus attention on discrete teaching skills and behaviors that can be improved. Unless a trusting relationship is established between the teachers working together as peer coaches, the person doing the teaching at any particular time will be unwilling to even recognize, much less acknowledge, areas for improvement, and little positive growth can be expected.

Assumption 4: Those engaging in peer coaching are knowledgeable about the cognitive aspects of teaching.

Peer coaches must have a strong foundation in the cognitive aspects of teaching and learning in order to establish credibility with their peer coaching partners. This is true because the quality of a teacher's performance in the classroom is based largely on the quality of the decisions the teacher makes while teaching and the thought processes that drive those decisions (Garmston in Sparks, 1990). By helping a teacher think through what happens during a teaching episode in the classroom, a thoughtful and enlightened colleague can enhance that teacher's cognitive processes. In addition, this enhancement can help improve teaching decisions, resulting in improved teaching behaviors. Without a strong foundation in the cognitive aspects of teaching, it is difficult for anyone to understand teaching or even to discuss teaching in a meaningful way. Teachers must be extremely confident in a colleagues's ability to help them understand and improve instruction if they are to be expected to work cooperatively toward this common goal.

It is important to note that although peer coaches must be perceived as very knowledgeable about the cognitive aspects of instruction, extensive knowledge about specific content of the various subject disciplines is not necessary. Peer coaching assumes that the teacher responsible for teaching is knowledgeable in the subject content; the peer coach may or may not be knowledgeable about a particular content area but is always very knowledgeable about the teaching process.

> *Assumption 5:* Sufficient resources, including time, are available to engage in the peer coaching process.

Peer coaching requires access to resources if it is to be practiced successfully. Staff development sessions, some means of coordination, incentives for participation, and a substantial amount of time may all be needed to one degree or another, depending on how a program is organized. In most cases, time seems to be the major concern of most teachers when it comes to successfully engaging in peer coaching. In addition to the time required for planning and conducting conferences, time must be allocated for classroom observations, as well as for reflecting on teaching and learning.

It is difficult to estimate with reasonable accuracy the time required to complete a full cycle of peer coaching. The time needed necessarily varies with the nature of the problem or innovation addressed by the peer coaches. However, a full cycle, addressing a typical problem routinely faced by teachers in the classroom, generally could be completed in 3 to 6 hours. This estimate does not include time spent by the teacher working to correct the problem once it has been identified, but rather the time expended in conferencing and observation.

The implementation of a new complex teaching methodology may necessitate that peer coaches cycle through the process several times, thereby significantly increasing the time commitment. Before engaging in peer coaching programs, school officials first must be willing to allocate to teachers the resources needed for peer coaching to be successful.

> *Assumption 6:* Peer coaching may not be an appropriate tool for use with all teachers.

Although most teachers certainly can benefit from peer coaching relationships with their colleagues, peer coaching is not something to be forced on those who are unwilling or, for other reasons, not ready to participate. As was noted in the previous chapter, teachers are at many different stages of professional development. The professional growth needs of novice teachers, for example, may be better served by mentoring arrangements, which are described later in this chapter. Other, more experienced teachers may never feel comfortable performing in front of their colleagues; still others may lack the commitment required to be an equal partner in a peer coaching relationship. One word of caution is called for here. Regardless of the circumstances, we feel strongly that highly directive approaches to promote instructional improvement should never be used between teacher colleagues. Highly directive approaches are best left to those in administrative roles, for such approaches can destroy collegiality among teachers.

What Is Peer Coaching, and How Does It Work?

The term *coaching* in relation to helping teachers grow professionally was perhaps used first by Joyce and Showers (1982) in describing a comprehensive approach to staff development employed to help teachers in a California school implement an alternative model of teaching. The elements in the staff development program included a study of the theoretical basis for the teaching method, observations by teachers of demonstrations given by experts in the methodology, a chance for individual teachers to practice the methodology in a protected setting, and teachers coaching one another as they worked to integrate the new methodology into their individual classrooms and personal teaching repertoires. Joyce and Showers did not use the term *peer* in relation to coaching, although they clearly favored peers—teachers working with teachers—to coach one another in the implementation of new methodologies.

According to Joyce and Showers, the coaching of teaching involves five major functions:

- provision of companionship,
- giving technical feedback,

- analysis of application: extending executive control,
- adaptation to students, and
- personal facilitation. (p. 6)

The provision of companionship provides personal support for teachers during the frequently difficult process of trying to learn and implement something new in their classrooms. It provides for mutual reflection and the sharing of problems and frustrations and serves as a vehicle for thinking through problems with another person. Companionship makes the technical learning process easier and more pleasurable because a teacher is not required to struggle through a complex learning process in isolation.

Provision for giving technical feedback allows peer coaching team members to learn to give and receive feedback as they implement new practices in their classrooms. For example, they can observe each other teaching and make sure that all parts of a new strategy have been used correctly and brought together in the way intended. The provision for technical feedback helps keep the teacher's mind on perfecting the new skills and working through problem areas because he or she is aware that a knowledgeable person is observing the teaching performance and will provide detailed information about how successfully teaching strategies have been used. The coach giving the feedback benefits in that it is frequently easier to spot problems and recognize solutions when someone else is teaching; the observer also learns vicariously while giving feedback to a colleague. By watching a colleague teach, the observer, too, can be exposed to exciting new methods and materials for teaching that he or she may not otherwise have been exposed to.

To transfer a new methodology into the classroom, it must also be transformed. Conditions in the classroom are frequently different from those in a controlled training environment. New approaches to teaching must be adapted to fit classroom situations; they must be practiced in context until the teacher has a thorough understanding of how they work, how they will fit into the existing repertoire of teaching behaviors, and how they can be adapted to students. "Analysis of application—extending executive control" is how Joyce and Showers described the way teachers figure out how and when to use new methodology and what the result will be. A major function of coaching is to assist the peer colleague in mutually making decisions that permit the effective transfer and integration of new ideas into the classroom.

Successful teaching requires successful student response. When something new is introduced in the classroom, the students must be helped to adjust to and take advantage of the innovation. A major function of the coach is to help the teacher read the responses of students to the methods being used in the classroom and make the adjustments required to help the students be even more successful. This task of teaching, adaption to students, is particularly important during the early stages of the implementation of innovations, when teachers tend to pay more attention to their own behaviors than they do to the responses of their students to those behaviors.

The final function of coaching is personal facilitation. Anything new requires practice before it will approach the required standards of excellence. A coach, therefore, is required, during the early stages of implementation, to help the teacher keep perspective, try different approaches even if the first attempts may not succeed, and most of all, feel good about himself or herself during the trial stage. Personal facilitation helps the teacher continue the new approach when the going gets tough and it would be more comfortable to revert to the familiar.

The Peer Coaching Process

As has already been mentioned, numerous models of peer coaching are being practiced across the country (Ackland, 1991). However, all of the models that are known and practiced include some process whereby teams of teachers observe one another on a regular basis and provide support, companionship, feedback, and assistance to each other. Most of the peer coaching programs reported in the literature share at least three common elements: (a) a preobservation conference, (b) an observation, and (c) a postobservation conference (Desrochers & Klein, 1990; Glatthorn, 1984; Mohlman et al., 1982; Phillips & Glickman, 1991). We therefore provide a detailed description of how teachers can effectively practice these three common elements of peer supervision to work with their colleagues toward instructional improvement.

Stage 1: Preobservation Conference

The peer coaching process is initiated with a preobservation conference between the teachers who have chosen to work together as a team. Although the peer coaching team may include three or more teachers, two seems to be the preferred arrangement. The preobservation conference is probably the most critical stage of the entire process because if the goals of the preobservation conference are not realized, then chances are that the rest of the process will not measure up to expectations. The purposes of the conference are to (a) establish communications and build trust between the team members, (b) provide the teacher an opportunity to "rehearse" his or her lesson with the coach, (c) enable the teacher and the coach to agree on the purpose for the intended observation, and (d) make arrangements for the coach to observe a class.

Assume, for a moment, that you are in the role of the coach. You should begin the preobservation conference by spending a few minutes attempting to relax your colleague by discussing topics of personal or general interest (e.g., school activities, vacation trips, news events). Remember, no matter how competent a person is, everyone has a tendency to be a little nervous when someone else, especially a fellow professional, is watching him or her perform a job. And as the coach, you can also expect to be a little nervous because you will want to measure up in the eyes of your colleague.

A typical opening for a preobservation conference might go something like this:

Coach: Good morning, Jim. I see you've already got your coffee. How was your weekend?

Teacher: Good, but busy. My son, Chris, is playing classic soccer this season, so we're required to travel out of town for matches on weekends.

Coach: Chris must be a very accomplished player. I've heard it's tough to get selected for one of those classic teams.

Teacher: It is pretty tough, but Chris works hard at his soccer. I wish he was half as dedicated to his studies.

Coach: Boy, do I know what you mean! Neither one of my children showed any inclination to study. I seriously doubted they would get through high school, much less go on to college. But tell me about the children I'm going to be seeing when I come to your classroom. Are most of them pretty serious about their studies?

We encourage you to take your time with this part of the preobservation conference. It is not necessary that you prolong this informal interaction beyond what is productive to achieve your purpose, but do not give the impression that you are trying to rush through the preliminaries so that you can get down to the business at hand. Take all the time you need for both you and your colleague to relax and feel comfortable with each other. Let your colleague know that you are genuinely interested in communicating on a personal, as well as a professional, level.

Once both parties are sufficiently at ease, you may focus the conference on instructional issues. This focus gives the person who will be doing the teaching an opportunity to rehearse the upcoming lesson by discussing with you (a) his or her goals and objectives for the lesson; (b) what he or she will do to achieve those goals and objectives; (c) how he or she expects the students to respond to the various materials, techniques, and procedures employed during the lesson; and (d) what he or she anticipates the payoff will be in terms of student learning. Through active listening and skilled questioning, you should attempt to elicit information from the teacher in all of these areas, thereby helping the teacher perform a "mental walk-through" of the lesson. This mental walk-through by you and the teacher may even result in some revisions to the teacher's plans if warranted by the discussion. We suggest that you use the following kinds of questions to help structure this part of the discussion:

1. Tell me about the makeup of your class. How many students are there? Are they unique in any way?
2. What will your students be learning about in the class I will visit?
3. What are the objectives for the lesson I will be observing?
4. How will you go about achieving your objectives? What techniques, methods, or materials will you use?
5. What techniques will you use to get and keep students involved?
6. How will you know whether the students have met your objectives?

These questions are intended to provide a general format for the discussion that needs to occur at this stage of the preobservation conference. Naturally, you could and should ask numerous other questions and invite questions from the teacher as a follow-up to the responses the teacher gives to the basic questions suggested above.

The third purpose of the preobservation conference is to allow the teacher and the coach to focus on the purpose or goals of the observation to take place. Without some mutual understanding of the purpose for the observation, the danger is that it will become ritualistic, with both players—the teacher and the coach—going through the motions with no particular end in mind except to get through the exercise. Does the teacher wish the coach to focus on a particular area of concern, such as his or her use of questioning skills or how student participation is encouraged or discouraged? Does the teacher want the coach to observe the lesson in a more global sense and to offer some specific areas for future concentration? Or perhaps the teacher may want to try a new approach in working with students and to have the coach observe and give feedback on the teacher's effectiveness in implementing the new approach. The following questions should prove useful in helping both you and the teacher focus on the purpose for the classroom observation that will follow in the next stage of the peer coaching process:

1. Do you have any special area of interest or a particular concern or problem on which you would like me to focus my attention during my visit in your classroom? (If the teacher expresses a problem or concern, you may ask the following questions.)

   a. What do you think might be causing the problem?
   b. Have you tried anything to address the problem? What did you try? What were the results?
   c. Do you have any additional ideas for addressing the problem?
   d. What do you think might happen if you tried to implement some of these ideas in your classroom?

(If the teacher has no particular areas of concern for you to focus on while observing, you might ask the following question.)

2. Because you have not expressed any particular problems or concerns you would like me to focus on at this time, would you like me to take a look at the class in a more holistic fashion and provide you with information about your teaching in a broader sense?

The important point to remember is that your job as a coach is to respond to the needs of the teacher. The teacher will govern the call concerning the purpose of the observation, but both of you need a clear understanding of what that purpose is and how it can be achieved during the observation to follow. In this way, you can gather appropriate data during the classroom observation, the data will be more likely to meet the expectations of both you and the teacher, and the results should be more useful for planning further instructional improvements for the teacher.

The final purpose of the preobservation conference is to make arrangements for your visit to the classroom to observe a lesson. By the way, we suggest that you use the term *visit*, rather than *observation*, given the negative feelings that have become associated with teachers being "observed" by a host of administrators over the years. Remember that classroom visits between peer coaching team members are never unannounced, as is frequently the case when teachers are observed by administrators or supervisors. Classroom visits between peers purposely are scheduled at the convenience of both the teacher and the coach.

The following questions should help guide you in structuring this part of the conference:

1. What day or days would be best for me to visit? What class period (or time) would you like me to spend with you?
2. Is there a particular place you'd prefer me to sit when I visit?
3. When would you like to get together to discuss the information I collect during my visit?
4. Do you have questions about my role or your role during the peer coaching process?

The goals of the preobservation conference should have been met now, and you can close the conference by thanking the teacher for his or her efforts to improve instruction and perhaps by telling the teacher that you are really looking forward to the opportunity to visit in the classroom. Again, at this stage of the peer coaching process, the tone of the relationship between the teacher and the coach is the most important consideration. What is said during the preobservation conference may not be as important as the feelings that are generated.

Stage 2: Observation

Even if you have been successful in conducting the preobservation conference, you should expect that the teacher still may experience some anxiety during the observation itself. You might use a number of strategies to reduce those anxieties. The first strategy is purely semantic but is significant nonetheless. As we already have suggested, in all of your conversations with your peer coaching team members, change the word *observation* to *visit*. *Observation* conjures up the image of the teacher being under a microscope where all his or her faults are revealed. *Visit*, however, suggests a mutually pleasant encounter that one should even look forward to experiencing.

The second strategy is for peer coaching teams to share on a regular basis their ideas about effective instruction, to discuss situations in which teachers are teaching effectively and children are learning at an optimal level. No matter what instructional improvement model is being used, teachers need to share and discuss with their colleagues the kinds of teaching behaviors that produce the learning results that everyone should want to achieve. This sharing is essential if teachers are to set high expectations for themselves and their students and, with the help of their colleagues, create a shared vision for effective teaching with which they can feel comfortable.

The third strategy is for peer coaching teams to visit each other's classrooms so often that their presence becomes routine and is thereby nonthreatening. The more you visit a colleague's classroom, the more likely you are to get an accurate picture of his or her typical performance and the more relaxed and receptive he or she is likely to be toward suggestions you may have for instructional improvements.

The fourth strategy you might use to reduce a peer's anxiety about classroom visits is to use visits for purposes other than observations. For example, visits might be used to help set up an experiment or special exercise, to evaluate curriculum, or even to assist with instruction. If you occasionally offer yourself as another pair of hands, you likely will find a colleague who is glad to welcome you into his or her classroom.

The two basic types of classroom observations are focused and unfocused. In a *focused observation*, the observer concentrates on specified teaching behaviors that have been agreed on during the preobservation conference. For example, if a teacher requests assistance with varying the types of questions he or she asks (higher order, as opposed to lower order), then the peer coach would conduct a tightly focused observation, perhaps recording only the questions the teacher asks students during the observed teaching segment. These questions then could be reviewed later and placed in categories for discussion by the coach and the teacher.

As a second example of a focused observation, suppose the teacher is concerned because only a few students are regularly involved in classroom discussions led by the teacher. If this concern is expressed during the preobservation conference, then the peer coach, with the teacher's approval, might collect data during the observation on the number and kinds (higher order vs. lower order) of questions asked by the teacher; the amount of time the teacher allows for students to respond to a question; the way the questions are asked (e.g., global, invitational, directed); which students have questions directed to them; and how the teacher reacts to students' responses to questions through the use of verbal and nonverbal reinforcers. In this second example, the observation is still focused, but the focus is broader than in the first example.

The second type of observation is the *unfocused observation*. In this type of observation, the peer coach and the teacher have not determined a specific focus for the observation, so the charge to the coach is to record as much data as possible about the total classroom experience. The most common approach used in the unfocused observation is *scripting*: The supervisor tries to record a script of the verbal interchanges that occur between the teacher and the students during the course of the lesson. When they first begin to work with a teacher for the first time, many peer coaches find it useful to conduct an unfocused observation of the teacher's classroom in order to help identify specific problem areas on which the teacher may want to focus his or her attention in the future. Once problem areas have been identified through the use of unfocused observations, however, then focused observations usually are conducted during subsequent observations as specific instructional problems are addressed.

When you are observing in a classroom, try to be as unobtrusive as possible. It is a good idea to arrive early and to station yourself where you can have an optimal view of the teacher and the students without drawing unnecessary attention to yourself. Usually your location in the classroom is one of the important details that have been mutually predetermined during the preobservation conference.

Once in the classroom, you should go about the business of collecting data. The choice of instrument used to collect the data should be based on the area of focus for the observation. If the observation is focused, the data collected should be specific to the area of interest. In most cases, the coach can construct a simple instrument to fit each particular situation. In general, the less complex the instrument, the better for all concerned.

If the observation is to be unfocused, however, you as the coach must attempt to record as much information as possible through scripting the lesson, writing as much as you can about what is said and done by teacher and students during the teaching episode. If the teacher has no objections, the coach even may audiotape or videotape the lesson, which can be reviewed together later. Although each peer coach will develop his or her own recording style, it is important that the data be detailed and specific. For example, you should attempt to record the actual words used by the teacher and the students.

After the observation has been completed, you should exit the classroom with as little notice as possible. We suggest that, if it is convenient to do so, you give your peer coaching colleague a few words of encouragement as you take your leave. For example, during the period between the class change, you might say something like, "That was fun! Thanks for letting me come. I think I will have some interesting data for us to consider together. See you tomorrow afternoon." If you have to leave when it is not convenient to speak with your colleague, leave a note or make a point to get back to him or her as soon as you possibly can. All educators are anxious when their colleagues watch them at work. Be very sensitive to this and make sure to give appropriate reinforcement at this critical time.

After the observation, you as the peer coach must review the data collected during the observation stage, analyze it, and plan the postobservation conference. If the observation was focused, you should review the data related to the area of concern and develop a plan for discussing it with the teacher. If the observation was unfocused, you should identify areas of concern, if they are present in the data, and develop a plan for presenting the data and discussing a selected area of concern with the teacher.

Although a peer coach may identify several areas of concern during an observation, it is generally not advisable to discuss multiple concerns during a single postobservation conference. During a focused observation, an area of concern has already been predetermined. During an unfocused observation, however, a number of areas of concern might emerge from the data. From the universe of concerns identified, the coach should determine the one most likely to have the greatest effect on student achievement and make this area the focus of the postobservation conference.

Just as teachers should have a lesson plan to teach a lesson, the peer coach should have a conference plan for the postobservation conference. The plan should include (a) objectives (What do I want my colleague to know or be able to do as a result of this conference?), (b) a set of procedures (What will I do to facilitate the teacher being able to meet the objectives?), and (c) an evaluation (How will I know whether the objectives have been met?). Once you as the coach have developed a suitable conference plan, then you are ready to conduct the postobservation conference.

Stage 3: The Postobservation Conference

The postobservation conference provides an opportunity for the coach and the teacher to discuss the recently observed teaching performance as colleagues. The purposes of the postobservation conference are to (a) present the teacher with the data gathered during the observation, (b) assist the teacher in understanding and interpreting the data, and (c) support and guide the teacher in formulating strategies to improve future teaching.

At this stage of the peer coaching process, you as the peer coach must be very careful not to give the impression that you have all of the answers, or even any of the answers, for that matter. Rather, as Wasley (1991) noted in the behavior of successful teacher leaders she studied, "They asked that teachers examine current practices against their hopes for their students, and then suggested additions to existing instructional repertoires" (p. 171).

As a peer coach, you should initiate a postobservation conference in much the same way as you would a preobservation conference—by engaging the teacher in friendly conversation about topics of common interest to set a supportive tone for the conference to follow, to further build trust, and to reduce teacher anxiety.

After you have accomplished these purposes, you will want to get the teacher to relive the lesson observed, to think through

what transpired during the teaching episode, and to be as introspective as possible. We think this can best be accomplished with
such questions as "Can you tell me some things you did during
the lesson that you think were effective in helping you achieve
your objectives?" and "How do you feel about the lesson you
invited me to observe? How well do you think it went?" This
approach generally provides a nice opening to the business at
hand and puts the teacher in the position of dealing with his or
her priorities first. Should the teacher be unable to recall any
positive behaviors or to express any opinions regarding the degree
of success of the lesson taught, you might prod the teacher by
using some of the data you collected. For example, you might say,
"Every student in your class was involved during the lesson. Do
you remember anything you did that caused this to happen?"

    If, after an extended period of time, only the positive features
of the teacher's lesson have been discussed during the conference
and the negative features ignored, you might try asking the
teacher, "If you could reteach this lesson, what could you do
differently to improve the results?" If the teacher has trouble
thinking of suggestions, try prodding the teacher by using specific data you collected during the observation. For example, you
might say, "After you distributed the worksheet to students, many
of the students began working, but seven or eight students asked
for individual assistance. Is there anything you might have done
before students began this assignment that would have prevented
so many students having questions about the assignment?"

    As a peer coach, you want to avoid being judgmental at all
costs. As Berliner so aptly put it, "What I exclude from coaching
is walking into the classroom and saying, 'You're deficient in
analytic questions. I'm going to tell you how to do it.' That strikes
me as the wrong way to work with professionals" (Berliner in
Brandt, 1982, p. 4). Rather than stating what is wrong and what to
do about it, you should strive to help your colleague discover
these things for himself or herself.

    As you guide the teacher toward thinking about what took
place during the lesson, you need to simultaneously reinforce the
positive behaviors that occurred and discourage less positive behaviors. As the teacher recalls specific behaviors that were effec-

tive, you will want to reinforce these behaviors and encourage the teacher to continue them; as negative behaviors are recalled, you will want to suggest, or better yet, guide the teacher in suggesting alternative behaviors that will lead to more positive results. Again, a series of questions can be used to effectively structure the discussion:

1. What kinds of things did students do while you were teaching that you didn't want them to do? How many did it? When did they do it? How often did these behaviors occur?
2. What would you prefer the students to have been doing?
3. Did you do anything (teaching behaviors) that might have contributed to the undesirable behaviors on the part of the students?
4. What might you do differently to alter the undesirable behaviors on the part of the students? As the teacher suggests various alternatives, ask, What would be the likely result if you tried that?

Handled correctly, this series of questions accomplishes several important purposes: (a) The teacher is encouraged to focus on a clearly defined area of concern; (b) the teacher can envision an alternative set of conditions in which the area of concern is no longer present; (c) the teacher is encouraged to try to link his or her teaching behaviors with student behaviors; and (d) the teacher is forced to consider what he or she might do differently to encourage the students, in turn, to respond differently.

Most important, the peer coaching process gives teachers useful practice in systematically thinking through and solving instructional problems. It encourages each individual teacher to take personal responsibility for assessing his or her own strengths and weaknesses and for coming up with effective means to address them. By using a carefully designed series of questions to structure the conferences with the teacher, the coach ensures that all of these things will happen. As teams of teachers develop a broader range of skills in instructional problem solving, they will have less need to rely on outside assistance to solve problems in their classrooms.

After all, helping teachers become independent problem solvers of instructional problems is the primary goal of peer coaching.

Ultimately, the postobservation conference should focus on a specific area of concern, if such a concern exists, so that teacher and coach can collaboratively think of ways and means to address the concern. Although a peer coach usually will enter into the postobservation conference with specific objectives that he or she would like to achieve, the coach must make every effort to allow the teacher to identify, analyze, and solve his or her instructional concerns with as little interference as possible. It is important, therefore, that the coach be prepared to provide the teacher specific data to substantiate where particular instructional concerns might be and to formulate questions that will make the teacher think about how his or her teaching behaviors affect student behaviors.

For example, instead of saying to a teacher, "It appears that you are experiencing a few classroom management problems," you might say the following:

> Although the class was scheduled to begin at 10:00, instruction did not actually start until 10:15. According to my notes, the first 15 minutes were spent checking the roll, handing out books, and waiting for the overhead projector to arrive from the media center. During this period, two students were arguing in the rear of the classroom, three had their heads down on their desks, and two more came in late. I know you are concerned about how time is used in your classroom. What specific actions might you take so that this situation could be prevented in the future?

Remember the power of questions in helping teachers focus on teaching behaviors and how those behaviors directly influence student behaviors.

The instructional improvement conference should end with the plan of action developed by the peer coaching team in response to the particular teaching problem that has been the focus of the entire cycle. The plan of action may be quite simple (e.g., the teacher will rearrange the chairs in the classroom from a row arrangement to a horseshoe arrangement in order to encourage students to discuss issues with each other). In other instances, the plan of action may be more complex, perhaps requiring the teacher to study materials on higher order questioning skills and then implement four or five variations on questioning techniques in the classroom. Regardless of the complexity of the plan of action, this portion of the conference should provide the resolution of an instructional problem that was identified as an area of concern either during the preobservation conference for a focused observation or during the analysis of a teaching segment by the peer coach after an unfocused classroom observation.

If both the teacher and the coach agree, then the proposed plan of action can set the stage for another peer coaching cycle. This addition may be appropriate if the teacher wants information about how effective the proposed plan of action will be in solving his or her instructional concerns. In such a scenario, the postobservation conference simultaneously serves as the subsequent preobservation conference for the next cycle, and plans are made for the peer coach to observe the teacher as he or she implements the plan of action during future lessons. The second peer coaching cycle then continues, with another observation, followed by another postobservation conference, and so on until the areas of concern have been sufficiently addressed.

At the conclusion of the peer coaching cycle, you as the peer coach should mentally review the entire process. You should analyze and evaluate all of your interactions with the teacher by asking yourself such questions as, What did I do that I think was effective in working with my colleague? What did I do that was ineffective? If I could do it all again, what would I do differently so that I could be even more effective in helping my colleague become a more independent and competent professional?

Although this review is informal, it provides you as the coach with an important opportunity for reflection, introspection, and professional growth. It gives you an opportunity to practice and reinforce exactly the same kinds of reasoning that you have been using with your teaching colleague to improve instructional performance.

Mentoring: A Special
Kind of Peer Coaching

Although mentoring is similar to peer coaching in many respects, there are some important differences. Unlike peer coaching, mentorship implies that one person is more knowledgeable in an area than another person. In the mentoring process, an older, more experienced teacher is paired with a novice teacher to provide assistance and support during the induction period that everyone must go through to become a professional teacher. Furthermore, as a result of the mentoring relationship, it is expected that the person being mentored will be the primary beneficiary of the arrangement, although this is not necessarily true. At the same time the novice is working to achieve autonomy and full professional status, the mentor may be growing in self-confidence while improving his or her knowledge and self-awareness about teaching. Regardless of whether or not each of the mentoring team members experiences equal benefits, the school and the students in the school ultimately benefit because the quality of instruction stands to be improved.

Improving instructional competence is the primary reason for establishing mentoring relationships. This is the reason that the peer coaching model is such a useful tool in mentoring programs. In mentoring, classroom observations do not necessarily have to be one-way, with only the experienced teacher observing the novice teacher; they can be two-way, just as they are in peer coaching. In fact, it is probably a very good thing to have the novice teacher observe the mentor from time to time and offer feedback, just as the mentor observes the novice and offers feedback. Both can learn a great deal from such an arrangement. The novice gains the advantage of an experienced person's view of what is happening in his or her classroom, and the mentor benefits from a fresh perspective on the happenings in his or her classroom.

Although some research has suggested that mentors have limited value and that teachers often look to professionals other than assigned mentors for assistance (Marso & Pigge, 1990), mentoring generally has been viewed as a valuable tool for helping inexperienced teachers move successfully into the profession (Odell, 1990). Heller (1991) suggested that mentors can perform many important functions to help novice teachers, including (a) increasing their professional competence; (b) serving as a resource on the art and craft of teaching, as well as on school policy and procedures; (c) increasing self-confidence; and (d) providing support and friendship. A *mentor* has been defined as a supporter, a trusted guide, a role model, a counselor, a developer of talent, and an opener of doors (Galvez-Hjornevik, 1986).

The effectiveness of mentoring programs depends almost entirely on the quality of the mentors. Significant skills and qualities are required of mentors. They must have good interpersonal skills. They must express a genuine caring about others and feel a responsibility for the professional development of their colleagues (Huling-Austin, 1992; Rauth & Bowers, 1986). *Openness, confidence, leadership, concern,* and *maturity* are all words commonly used in describing the successful mentor (Healy & Welchert, 1990; Huling-Austin, 1992; Odell, 1990). And, most important, the mentor must be a highly skilled, respected, and effective teacher.

The need for quality training is just as important to the success of mentoring programs as it is to peer coaching programs in general. Mentors may need to receive training in areas of immediate concern to beginning teachers, such as lesson planning, effective instructional techniques, and classroom management. Mentors also can benefit from training in the special nature of mentoring relationships, observational strategies, and adult learning.

Now that we have addressed the essential elements of peer coaching and the special nature of mentoring, we turn our attention to how these programs can be implemented in schools by teacher leaders.

How to Get a Peer Coaching Program Started

A number of logistical considerations must be taken into account when planning and implementing a peer coaching program.

What follows is a brief outline of the most important questions that need to be addressed in order to get a peer coaching program up and running.

1. Who Will Assume Leadership for
Getting the Program Started and
Directing It Once It Is Established?

In most situations, it is probably best that a team of teachers, administrators, and other staff members be used as a vehicle to provide the leadership for getting a peer coaching program started. A team approach is best for several reasons: (a) It provides a broad basis for communication about and promotes understanding of peer coaching and its purposes; (b) it helps ensure that the needed resources are allocated to make the program successful; and (c) it makes feasible the necessary logistical arrangements needed to implement the program, such as common planning time for teachers working in the same teams. Although administrators can be very helpful in planning and assisting during the initial stages of the implementation of a peer coaching program, it is much better for the program to be coordinated and directed by teachers once it is established. This approach may necessitate some released time for teacher leaders with coordination responsibilities.

2. What Will Be the Scope of the
Program, and Who Will Be Involved?

Peer coaching programs have been used for a variety of purposes, including the introduction of both programmatic and instructional innovations in schools, as well as for curriculum development purposes and general instructional improvement based on teams of teachers coaching one another by giving feedback on classroom observations. The leadership team needs to decide what to include under the guise of peer coaching and who will take part. The overwhelming consensus is that as many teachers as wish to do so in a school may participate, but participation should be on a voluntary basis.

3. Who Will Work With Whom, and How Large Should Peer Coaching Teams Be?

Many schools have policies that require the survey of teachers to determine their preferences for peer coaching partners. Teachers may list as many preferences as they wish, and the person or persons with the responsibility for coordinating the program then can sort out the requests and finalize the teams with the consent of the participants. It does not seem to matter whether peer coaches teach the same grade or even the same subject. The major consideration is that the people involved want to work together. Teams of two or three teachers are preferred, but larger teams have functioned well in some situations.

4. How Will the Teachers Be Trained in the Techniques of Coaching, and Who Will Coach the Coaches?

A considerable amount of training generally is required to ensure that a peer coaching program has a reasonably good chance of success. At a minimum, teachers who will be participating in peer coaching will need a thorough orientation to the philosophy and guiding principles underlying peer coaching, as well as training in techniques for observing in classrooms, gathering data, and providing productive feedback. If peer coaching is being used to introduce major innovations such as new programs or new teaching methodologies, then additional training centered on the planned innovations also will be required. The training may be done by internal staff members if appropriate expertise is available, or experts may be brought in from the outside to do the training. If outside expertise is required, then financial resources must be set aside for this purpose.

5. Will Incentives Be Provided for
Teachers Who Participate in the Program,
and How Will Incentives Be Provided?

The opportunity to participate in peer coaching is an incentive itself. Being able to share problems and concerns with a fellow professional in a nonthreatening and supportive atmosphere and to improve one's ability to perform at a higher level may be the only incentives most teachers need for participating in peer coaching. However, if teachers are required to attend training sessions during off-time or to engage in activities related to peer coaching beyond the normal school day, then some incentives for participation may need to be considered. At a minimum, teachers should be provided time away from their class responsibilities to observe their peers and to engage in conferences. This provision may require the use of substitute teachers to cover classes from time to time and scheduling considerations that give peer coaching teams common free periods from teaching responsibilities.

6. How Will the Program Be Evaluated?

The nature of the program will guide how it may be evaluated. If peer coaching is being used to introduce a schoolwide innovation, then the success of the program implementation may well form the basis for the evaluation. For example, the evaluation may examine the strategies teachers employ in the classroom before and after peer coaching. An evaluation may be based on a survey of teacher attitudes toward themselves, their teaching, their colleagues, and their students. These variables even could be linked with student achievement data or with student satisfaction as outcome variables. Many factors can be reflective of the success or failure of a program. Teacher participants in peer coaching will need to decide which of these factors should be used to measure the results of the program.

The Value of Peer Coaching

Peer coaching is an intensive collaborative process that encourages teachers working with teachers on a one-on-one, highly professional basis. To practice peer supervision effectively, teacher leaders must embrace a philosophy that supports the concept of teachers working together as colleagues to improve instruction. The primary goal of peer coaching is to help teachers improve instruction by teaching them to become independent instructional problem solvers. This goal is best accomplished by creating a supportive, nonthreatening collegiality among teachers, characterized by the application of techniques that encourage teachers to become more introspective about how their teaching behaviors influence student behaviors in the classroom.

Peer coaching has proven its effectiveness in breaking down barriers among teachers and in making them equal partners in instructional improvement. Peer coaching has been an effective means to get teachers talking with other teachers about teaching, just as doctors have long talked with their colleagues about medicine. It has reduced feelings of isolation among teachers, increased collegiality and professional dialogue, and developed renewed feelings of self-esteem, professionalism, and respect that are congruent with increasingly higher levels of teacher involvement and teacher empowerment. Peer coaching has been instrumental in giving everyone involved a significant share of the responsibility for what happens both in classrooms and in schools in general. In short, where it has been used, peer coaching has helped make teachers and teaching more professional.

9

Reform, Restructuring, and Renewal

The Critical Need for Teacher Leadership

According to Benjamin Franklin, "In this world nothing can be said to be certain, except death and taxes" (Bartlett, 1882/1992, p. 310). To this, we would add a third certainty: criticism of the American educational system. Three examples serve to illustrate this third certainty.

In 1930, a commission was formed to "consider ways by which the secondary schools of the United States might better serve all our young people" (Alkin, 1942, p. 1). The commission issued a report, based on more than a year of study, in which secondary education was found to be "clearly inadequate in certain major aspects of its work" (Alkin, 1942, p. 1). Specifically,

> Secondary education . . . did not have a clear-cut, definite, central purpose. . . .

Schools neither knew their students well nor guided them wisely. . . .

Schools failed to create conditions necessary for effective learning. . . .

The conventional high school curriculum was far removed from the real concerns of youth. . . .

The traditional subjects of the curriculum had lost much of their vitality and significance. . . .

[There was] little evidence of unity in the work of the typical high school. Subjects and courses had been added until the program, especially of large schools, resembled a picture puzzle, without consistent plan or purpose. (Alkin, 1942, pp. 3-5)

In the 1960s, a rash of critics appeared on the American educational scene. Among the most vocal were John Holt, Ivan Illich, and Charles Silberman. In his classic *Crisis in the Classroom*, Silberman (1970) summarized much of the criticism in vogue at that time.

The public schools are failing dismally in what has always been regarded as one of their primary tasks—in Horace Mann's phrase, to be "the great equalizer of the conditions of men," facilitating the movement of the poor and disadvantaged into the mainstream of American economic and social life. Far from being "the great equalizer," the schools help perpetuate the differences in condition, or at the very least, do little to reduce them. . . .

This failure is not new; it is one the United States has tolerated for a century or more. The public school never has done much of a job educating youngsters from the lower class or from immigrant homes. For one thing, as Lawrence A. Cremin has pointed out, we have greatly exaggerated the "commonness" of the common school, which has always been essentially a middle-class or upper middle-class institution. (pp. 53-54)

In the early 1980s, yet another commission was formed—the National Commission on Excellence in Education (NCEE). After much study, this commission presented its findings in a report titled *A Nation at Risk: The Imperative for Education Reform* (1983). Apparently unaware of the long-standing criticism of American education, the authors of the report wrote:

> Our Nation is at risk. Our once unchallenged preeminence in commerce, industry, science, and technological innovation is being overtaken by competitors throughout the world. . . . We report to the American people that while we can take justifiable pride in what our schools and colleges have historically accomplished and contributed to the United States and the well-being of its people, the educational foundations of our society are presently being eroded by a rising tide of mediocrity that threatens our very future as a Nation and a people. What was unimaginable a generation ago has begun to occur— others are matching and surpassing our educational attainments. If an unfriendly foreign power had attempted to impose on America the mediocre educational performance that exists today, we might well have viewed it as an act of war. (p. 2)

One can debate the validity of these criticisms (the extent to which they were supported by the evidence available at the time). For example, contrary to the NCEE assertion that "others matching and surpassing our educational attainments" was "unimaginable a generation ago," there were beliefs as early as 1957, with the launching of *Sputnik* by the then Soviet Union, and "hard data" available as early as 1967 (Husen, 1967) that students in the United States were lagging in mathematics achievement in comparison with their counterparts in other countries.

One cannot debate, however, the impact of these criticisms on American education. The 1930 commission report provided the basis for the Progressive Education movement (Informal Committee, 1942). The criticisms of the 1960s led to numerous curriculum development and redesign efforts (Tanner & Tanner, 1975). Finally, the 1983 NCEE report led to a whole host of attempts to change and, ostensibly, improve American education (Carnegie Foundation for the Advancement of Teaching, 1986).

Although in most cases the responses to these criticism have been swift, none have led to substantial, meaningful, and long-lasting change in American education (Cuban, 1984b) or to a substantial reduction in the number or vociferousness of the critics. Why is this so? Our answer is quite simple and straightforward: These efforts to improve education have focused on reform and restructuring, rather than on renewal.

School Reform and Restructuring

To understand the failure of school reform and restructuring efforts, one needs to understand the meaning of these terms. *School reform* means to change elements *within* the existing school structure; that is, the current structure of schools is accepted as a "given." As a consequence, school reform proponents focus on raising standards for attendance, behavior, and achievement; revising the curriculum of various subject matters (e.g., science, social studies); altering the ways various subject matters are taught (e.g., whole language vs. phonics approach to teaching reading); increasing graduation requirements for high school students; changing the ways students are assigned to classrooms (e.g., heterogeneous vs. homogenous grouping); mandating formal evaluations of teachers; and requiring teachers to upgrade their knowledge and skills to retain their certification. Unfortunately, little evidence suggests that school reform efforts are effective (Fullan & Stiegelbauer, 1991).

In contrast with school reform, *school restructuring* implies that the ways schools are organized and operate will be changed. In fact, *restructuring* is a term that implies the rules, roles, and relationships within an organization are changed. Thus, proponents of school restructuring debate such issues as graduation requirements (e.g., Carnegie units, exit examinations), the role of teachers in decision making (e.g., decisions on curriculum and instructional strategies), and the relationship of school district administrators and school administrators (e.g., centralization vs. decentralization). They argue about the relationship between state agencies and local school districts (e.g., whether school districts and schools should be regulated or deregulated). They discuss the merits of participatory decision making and site-based management. They suggest that teachers be empowered to make and implement decisions and that parents have greater input into school decision making by way of school improvement councils and similar associations and organizations. Although school restructuring efforts do not have the long history that school reform efforts do, little, if any, evidence suggests that school restructuring efforts are effective.

Although several reasons can be given for the failure of reform and restructuring efforts to significantly and substantially improve schools, one reason stands out. Just as morality cannot be legislated, change cannot be mandated. About 20 years ago, Rothkopf (1976) reminded us that students have absolute veto power over their learning; that is, neither teachers nor administrators can *cause* students to learn. Rather, students must be involved and engaged in the process of learning; in essence, they must learn for themselves. This fact does not diminish the responsibility of teachers and administrators; it merely changes it. The primary responsibility of teachers and administrators with respect to student learning is to create intellectually appropriate and socially and emotionally supportive "conditions of learning" (Gagne, 1974).

Like students, teachers and administrators (particularly building-level administrators) have absolute veto power over educational change, a power they use frequently. This veto power may be exercised in a variety of ways. It is noteworthy, however, that, with the exception of organized action on the part of teacher associations or unions, it is least likely to be exercised in *direct* opposition to mandates or regulations.

One of the more common methods by which teachers use their veto power is through passive resistance. Teachers simply may refuse to comply with the mandated change, reminding those in positions of authority that they are tenured and reminding themselves that "this too shall pass." Other teachers may agree with the change in principle but have difficulty with the way the change is being implemented. Still other teachers may simply ignore the change and go on with their own business. In each case, the teachers may smile blandly when the change is introduced and then, once safely behind the classroom door, do whatever he or she wants to do. When the principal enters this inner sanctum, the teacher, in effect, puts on a show.

In contrast, teachers may actively resist administrative mandates. These teachers may critically examine the proposed changes and decide that the result of such change would be no better than the status quo. Such teachers understand that covering material is more important than having students master the material they cover. They also understand that students, like teachers, balk at change; that is, maintaining the status quo is more "comfortable." Change involves risk, and students may not be willing to take those risks.

Likewise, administrators have a variety of tools to combat externally imposed change. One of the most common (and one they are often taught in their administrator preparation programs) is creative insubordination. One of the tenets of creative insubordination is that it is better to seek forgiveness than to ask permission. Thus, like teachers, administrators react to mandated change by doing what they wish and then asking (and usually receiving) forgiveness when they are "caught."

Teachers and administrators also may resist change because they truly believe that "change is bad." In the words of John Gardner (1964), "A common stratagem of those who wish to escape the swirling currents of change is to stand on high moral ground. They assert that the old way is intimately bound up in moral and spiritual considerations that will be threatened by any change" (p. 60).

Finally, some teachers and administrators may be more interested in "covering their tails" than in doing what is best for the clients or constituents. In common parlance, they have vested interests in the status quo. As Gardner asserted, vested interests "are among the most powerful forces producing rigidity and diminishing capacity for change. And these are the diseases of which organizations and societies die" (p. 66).

In addition, teachers may be held accountable for their actions. Unlike responsibility, which implies "you can trust me," accountability implies "you cannot trust me and therefore you must watch me at every turn." Virtually all people who find themselves in an accountability framework will do whatever is necessary to minimize their losses. They may, for example, limit the information they give to those who request it or establish standards that are so low that success will be guaranteed.

The problem with both reform and restructuring efforts, then, is that the reason or need for change comes from *outside* those who must make the change. When an external change is presented to teachers, they often lack the commitment needed to make the change happen (Firestone & Pennell, 1993). And, without commitment, as we have suggested, administrators and teachers have a multitude of weapons with which to resist externally imposed changes.

The Need for Renewal

We begin as we did in our discussion of school reform and renewal, with a definition of terms. Like reform and restructuring, *renewal* is also concerned with change. However, renewal differs from reform and restructuring in two important aspects. First, *renewal* is a change *within* people (and *within* organizations); that is, renewal is a change that is internally motivated rather than externally imposed. More specifically, renewal pertains to changes in the beliefs, values, motivations, interests, and concerns of those who live and work within the organization. The basic premise here is that people renew themselves; they are not renewed by others (particularly those who mandate or legislate that they must change).

Second, renewal is not coercive change ("You must change or else"); rather, it is change by choice, by desire, by will. As a consequence, change initiated by renewal is more likely to be passionate change, meaningful change, sustained change. This is precisely the type of change that teacher leaders can facilitate. Furthermore, as we discuss later, this type of change is essential in attempts to improve the schools.

Coercive change, in fact, destroys the possibility of renewal. It typically is legislated or mandated change. As a consequence, it is accompanied by many laws, regulations, policies, and the like. And, as Gardner reminded us, "One consequence of the proliferation of rules, customs and procedures is the bottling up of energy or, more accurately, the channeling of energy into all the tiny rivulets of conformity. The long process of mastering the rules smothers energy and destroys all zest, spontaneity or creativity" (p. 59).

Renewal can be defined also in terms of its opposite: burnout. A person who lacks energy, zest, spontaneity, and creativity is said to be "burned out." Interestingly, teachers hear more in the educational literature about burnout than they do about renewal. One fairly simple reason for this is that there are more opportunities for teacher burnout than there are for teacher renewal.

Maslach, Jackson, and Schwab (1986) defined *burnout* as the behavioral response of people who experience constant stress from working in occupations that require continual, intensive interactions with people. Those who cannot effectively cope with this work-related stress develop feelings of emotional exhaustion, negative attitudes toward their clients, and a sense that they no longer are accomplishing anything worthwhile in their jobs. In the context of this discussion, such people are badly in need of renewal. They need to feel energized by their students (rather than sapped of their energy by them). They need to perceive their students positively (rather than dread each encounter with them). They need to believe they can make a difference in their students' lives (rather than resign themselves to the fact that their success with students is constrained by the families from which their students come). This is the stuff of renewal. Unfortunately, administrators often either intentionally or unintentionally restrict teacher opportunities for renewal. The term *unfortunate* is used in this discussion because the education community can ill afford to lose any teacher, especially the most capable ones.

Why is renewal important? Several reasons can be given. First, renewal is a largely untapped resource. As Sirotnik (1987) pointed out, "The biggest day-to-day repository of constructive power to improve schools is in the hearts, minds, and hands of the people who work in them. It is my view that, under the right conditions and circumstances, this resource could be endlessly tapped" (pp. 43-44). The education community cannot afford to lose any teachers.

Second, school improvement depends totally and completely on the renewal of individual teachers and administrators. No meaningful, long-lasting school improvement can occur without renewal. As Gardner (1964) wrote, "Societies [e.g., schools] are renewed—if they are renewed at all—by people who believe in something, care about something, stand for something" (p. 143). Educators must ask themselves the following questions: What do we believe in? What do we care about? What do we stand for? Educators who cannot answer these questions are quite likely in the wrong field.

School Renewal and Student Learning

We can argue the importance of school renewal from at least two perspectives. To this point in the chapter, we have argued from the perspective of the adults who inhabit the schools— namely, teachers and administrators. A second perspective, however, is that of the students. Students neither need nor deserve burned-out teachers; rather, they need teachers who are enthusiastic, who "live to teach," who communicate to their students their own love of learning, and who model what they believe (in the vernacular, who "practice what they preach").

Too much emphasis has been given to the techniques, methods, and strategies of teaching. In contrast, too little emphasis has been given to the personalized aspect of teaching, what Jackson (1989) referred to as the "transformative nature of teaching." Jackson contrasted the transformative with the mimetic. Teachers operating within the mimetic (or imitative) framework focus on transmitting knowledge and skills to students. The mimetic approach works from the outside in; that is, knowledge and skills exist outside the students, and the job of the teacher is to get that knowledge and those skills into the students. In contrast, teachers operating within the transformative framework focus on transforming students' lives. They desire to help students see things in different ways, to question what students take for granted so that students can grow and develop. Transformative teachers work from the inside out.

We know an easy way to remember the difference between the mimetic and transformative perspectives. The teacher operating within the mimetic framework attempts to make the *unfamiliar familiar*. Thus, much of the teaching that occurs at the lower grade levels is mimetic because most of what students are expected to learn is unfamiliar to them (e.g., the incredibly arbitrary convention we call the alphabet; the names we attach to the things we experience so that we may communicate with others; the rules of our mathematical system).

In contrast, the teacher operating within the transformative framework is concerned with *making the familiar unfamiliar*—questioning basic assumptions, suggesting several ways to look at a particular issue or situation, helping students see the world in different ways. Somewhere along the educational continuum, every student needs to encounter at least one teacher who operates within the transformative framework. Such a teacher is quite likely to be one who periodically engages in renewal.

Teachers and School Renewal

How important are teachers in school renewal? In a word, central. What conception of teachers is needed to fulfill this role? In a phrase, teachers as professionals. That is, for schools to be renewed, teachers must see themselves as real and active members of a true profession. Furthermore, administrators and university personnel must recognize teaching as a profession.

Before teaching can be classified as a true profession, however, it must meet several criteria. First, an accepted body of knowledge must guide teaching practice. Second, within this body of knowledge must be a broad range of autonomy for both the individual teacher and teachers as a group. Third, acceptance of personal responsibility for judgments made and acts performed within the scope of professional autonomy must be the norm. Fourth, a comprehensive, self-governing organization of teachers must be included (Lieberman, 1956). We consider each of these criteria in turn.

An Accepted Body of Knowledge

No profession exists without an accepted body of knowledge. Dentists cannot do what "seems reasonable at the time." They cannot dismiss new research evidence because "the research was conducted on dentists in Louisiana and I am a dentist in Oregon" (an excuse that educators often use). Rather, as members of the dental profession, they must perform their duties in accordance with what is known in the field and the principles of "best practice." Similarly, attorneys are expected to know case law and court procedures. They also must adhere to principles such as representing the best interests of their clients and maintaining client confidentiality. Why are teachers any different?

Our suggestion that a body of knowledge exists is not intended to imply that this body of knowledge is universal. Rather, it is likely context specific. But the context does not necessarily include geographic boundaries (e.g., Louisiana, Oregon). It pertains to those conditions within which the knowledge is applicable. Some of these conditions are, in fact, geographic. For attorneys, laws do vary from state to state. Other conditions, however, are defined in terms of the clients being served. Orthodontic prescriptions for young children may be quite different from those given to adults. Similarly, the body of knowledge for teaching elementary students may be quite different from that for adult learners. The point here is simple: Any practicing professional must operate within the context of some acceptable, shared body of knowledge. He or she does not have license to close the door and do what he or she, personally, believes to be correct or right.

Many teachers are reluctant to endorse a body of knowledge. These teachers argue that teaching is an art, not a science. They do not want to be "constrained" by a body of knowledge; they want to "do their own thing." In fact, all professions are both science and art. Doctors have mastered certain techniques, while at the same time they have quite different bedside manners.

In fact, Dewey (1929) argued that science provides the basis for art. In his words, scientific knowledge "render[s] the performance of the educational function [practice, art] more enlightened, more ·humane, more truly educational than it was before" (p. 76).

Teachers who argue against the existence of a common body of knowledge often base their argument on the existence of different teaching styles. Their battle cry is "Not all teachers teach the same way." That is quite true. In fact, it is difficult to refute. But it is equally true that not all dentists "dentist" the same way. At the same time, this recognition does not excuse dentists from operating from the same body of knowledge.

Where does this body of knowledge originate? There are three primary sources. One source is research conducted in the field. Teachers should be aware of the major research findings. This is not to suggest that they spend a great deal of time reading original research studies. It does suggest that they are familiar with research summaries contained in such journals as *Educational Leadership, Review of Educational Research, Phi Delta Kappan,* and *Journal of Teacher Education.*

A second source is expert agreement; that is, if the "best" in the field agree on an issue, their agreement quite likely constitutes "best practice." Clearly, without a great deal of evidence to the contrary, consensus among experts is an excellent source. At the same time, one would expect that experts' expertise depends to a certain extent on existing data.

A third source, and the one most related to this book, is accumulated knowledge that is passed from one generation to another. Interestingly and importantly, however, this source quite likely encompasses the prior two; that is, what is passed down from generation to generation is part empirical evidence and part expert agreement. Most teachers rely on this third source early in their careers as they make the transition from college student to public or private school teacher. They listen to their college teachers, they watch their student teaching supervisors, and they remember those who taught them as elementary and secondary students. From this information and misinformation, they decide what they value, what they will teach, and how they will teach.

In the context of this discussion, the source of this knowledge is far less important than the fact that this knowledge exists, is available, and is used to guide the decisions made and the actions taken by teachers. In fact, in loosely coupled organizations such as schools (Weick, 1976) and with increased demands to develop more complex and intellectually demanding approaches to teaching (Firestone & Pennell, 1993), a sound, defensible knowledge base for teachers may be more important now than it has ever been.

At the very least, teacher leaders have the responsibility for ensuring their teaching colleagues are aware of the existing body of knowledge that guides and informs their teaching. They also may wish to engage in discussions of the knowledge base with other teachers: What do we know? What do we think we know? How do we act on this knowledge (or lack thereof)? All of these questions are worthy of discussion on a regular basis.

Exercising this responsibility is especially important when dealing with beginning or novice teachers. Teacher leaders may be advised to periodically remind those experienced teachers who have focused so much internally that they may have forgotten about their membership in and responsibility to the teaching profession.

A Broad Range of Autonomy

Autonomy is a two-edged sword. Quite clearly, teachers need the freedom to do what needs to be done to accomplish what they need to accomplish. In most professions, there are more questions than answers. Furthermore, most of the answers that teachers are given are based on conditional, rather than absolute, knowledge; that is, the veracity of this knowledge depends on the presence of certain conditions; it does not hold "across the board."

Teachers are quick to point out that much of what they teach elementary and secondary students is conditional knowledge. They teach that water boils at 212 degrees Fahrenheit, and only later tell the students that this is a "fact" only at sea level. Likewise, teachers teach that the shortest distance between two points is a straight line (without always telling the students that this "truism" holds only within two-dimensional space).

Thus, for teachers, freedom is an absolute necessity. However, teachers should not have the license to do what they wish to do regardless of the consequences. The line between freedom and license is fine indeed. Teachers are well aware of the dual nature of autonomy. On the one hand, many appreciate and enjoy their freedom to close their doors and keep others out. They resent administrative intrusions and are reluctant to engage in team teaching situations. One of the primary reasons given for the use of teacher aides, rather than certified teachers, in Chapter I programs is that the threat to the primary teacher's authority is minimized with teacher aides (Anderson & Pellicer, 1990).

On the other hand, teachers often complain that they are isolated. And, for many teachers, with isolation comes disenchantment and alienation (Anderson, 1987a). Perhaps because of their isolation, disenchantment, and alienation, these teachers assert that no one seems to know or care about what they are doing or accomplishing (Ginsberg & Bennett, 1981). At the risk of being obvious, it seems reasonable to assume that the more you keep people out, the less these people will know or care about what you are doing.

Unfortunately for the entire teaching profession, a few teachers value their right to do what they wish over their responsibility to do what is right. Certainly, this is not a new development. As Bidwell (1965) pointed out about three decades ago, "The teacher works alone within the classroom, relatively hidden from colleagues and superiors, so that he [or she] has a broad discretionary jurisdiction within the boundaries of the classroom" (p. 976). Teacher leaders must help such teachers become aware of the intricate balance between freedom and license, between rights and responsibilities.

An Acceptance of Responsibility

Members of a profession assume responsibility for their judgments, their actions, and the consequences of both. This responsibility is based on a shared sense of commitment and value. As Firestone and Pennell (1993) pointed out, a "profession requires a deep commitment by all members that goes beyond pecuniary gain and requires the adoption of specific values" (p. 492). In fact, if teachers do not assume this responsibility, they are likely to be held accountable by those outside the profession.

The relationship of responsibility to accountability is a tenuous one, but one that is quite clear in education when the events of the past half century are examined. The launching of *Sputnik* in the late 1950s convinced those outside the educational establishment that educators were not acting responsibly. As a result, accountability measures pertaining to educational evaluation were built into the Elementary and Secondary Education Act of 1964, as well as the National Defense Education Act of 1965.

During the latter part of the 1970s and the early 1980s, the extent to which American teachers and administrators assumed responsibility for student learning was again called into question. The reaction—accountability legislation!

The distinction between accountability and responsibility is far more than semantic. The best description of the differences between the two concepts is provided by Sirotnik (1985). His distinction is similar to that between external and internal sources of change made earlier. Sirotnik wrote:

> For me . . . the current wave of reform is no more alarming or depressing now than at any other point during the last twenty years or so that I, at least, have been consciously attuned to the educational scene. It's just more of the same, and I mean "more," literally—more time, more homework, more courses, more testing, more standards . . . more *accountability*. (p. 3)

How do accountability and responsibility differ? Sirotnik (1985) answered in the following way.

> [We cannot] tinker around with what exists. I have come to the view that nothing short of reconceptualization and

TABLE 9.1 Some Heuristics for Shifting From Accountability to Responsibility

Replace	With
Produce	Process
Trade (worker)	Profession (professional)
Symbols (explanations)	Meanings (understandings)
Short-term	Long-term
Closure	Ambiguity
Confirmation	Exploration
Uniform	Contextual
Reactive	Proactive
Authority	Leadership
Isolation	Collaboration
Manipulation	Facilitation
External reward	Internal motivation
Legitimate right	Trust
Followership	Working consensus
Talk/conversation	Discourse/communication
Cost-benefit analysis	Critical analysis

> reconstruction would be anything else but rearranging the deck chairs on the *Titanic*. We must seriously rethink . . . what goes on in schools for students and, therefore, in schools for educators as well . . . [We must replace] "accountability" with the notion of *responsibility*. (p. 7)

Definitionally speaking, responsibility adds words such as *moral, trustworthy,* and *rational* to our meaning of accountability. It moves from external authority to internal obligation.

To further explicate his distinction, Sirotnik offered a set of heuristics. These heuristics are shown in Table 9.1. Several of the differences shown are noteworthy. In thinking about a teaching profession, teachers need to replace short-term with long-term, closure with ambiguity, uniform with contextual, authority with leadership, external reward with internal motivation, and legitimate right with trust. If these changes in thinking cannot be made, then meaningful changes in teachers' actions are impossible.

Teacher leaders are central in facilitating the shift from account-ability to responsibility.

A Comprehensive, Self-Governing Organization

If a profession of teaching is be realized, then teachers must real-ize that leadership comes with the territory. Fullan and Stiegelbauer (1991) reminded us that research on change suggests that the con-version to new instructional approaches requires many months, perhaps years, of extra work and discomfort. Thus, teachers need some credible reason for making the change if they are to expend the time and effort needed to make a successful change. Further-more, teachers must either be committed to the change (Firestone & Pennell, 1993) or be provided with incentives that will make the change worthwhile.

Although both incentives and commitment may produce the desired result, one once again is confronted with the difference between externally and internally imposed change. Thus, al-though incentives may produce short-term gains, commitment is needed to produce and sustain long-term gains.

The concept of self-governance implies that teachers need to see themselves as forming school culture, rather than as being formed by it. Some teachers see themselves as victims; they readily admit they are less effective than they could be but cite external reasons for this lack of effectiveness (McLaughlin et al., 1986). Individual teachers may be victims, but teachers as a collectivity certainly are not. Thus, teachers have no choice but to band to-gether. But, by banding together, they are not protecting them-selves; they are advancing the quality of education they provide their students. Again, teacher leadership is crucial.

The movement to a true teaching profession will not be an easy one. Teachers value their independence and their individuality. As Parish and Arends (1983) wrote:

It is well known that norms exist in schools that promote teacher autonomy and individualism. This means that most teachers cope with everyday teaching tasks . . . indi-

vidually, that they are prone *not* to interfere with the work
of colleagues, and that for the most part they guard carefully their right to teach in the ways they think best. (p. 63)

Nonetheless, without a teaching profession, teacher and school
renewal is virtually impossible.

The Stability Needed for Change

Many people see stability and change as polar opposites
(Bloom, 1965). This is not our point of view. Rather, we believe that
stability is necessary for change to occur in any meaningful, long-
lasting way. Change involves risk; risk taking is more likely to
occur in a stable environment. Change involves discomfort (Fullan
& Stiegelbauer, 1991); a stable environment can minimize feelings
of discomfort. Change requires hard work (Fullan & Stiegelbauer,
1991); a stable environment can provide the support needed to
sustain hard work.

Who holds the keys to the creation of a stable school environment? Teachers! Administrators come and go. The average tenure
of a school superintendent may be 4 or 5 years and of a building
principal, 6 to 7 years. The average duration of an innovative program is less than 10 years. In contrast, the average length of service
of a teacher in a school is far more than 10 years. Teachers—not
administrators, not programs—provide the stability in schools,
the stability needed to promote and sustain change.

Two constraints must be placed on our use of the word *teachers*
in the previous sentence. First, *teachers* is a collective noun; no
individual teacher can provide the stability needed for change.
Like administrators, individual teachers come and go. But teachers, collectively, live on within each school. Second, teachers are
professionals. As such, they operate within a knowledge base; they
make professional judgments consistent with that knowledge base;
they assume responsibility for themselves, their students, and
their colleagues (when they are allowed to do so); and they are
committed to their profession (they will do whatever is necessary
to maintain professional ethics and standards).

This book can be summarized as a syllogism. Leadership is needed for meaningful, sustained school change. Because of the stability they lend to schools, teachers are uniquely situated to provided the needed leadership. Therefore, teachers are critical in any effort to initiate and sustain educational change. Is teacher leadership the best answer to the problems confronting education? It may not be the best answer—but it is the only one.

References

Ackland, R. (1991). A review of the peer coaching literature. *Journal of Staff Development, 12*(1), 22-27.

Alkin, W. (1942). *The story of the eight-year study.* New York: Harper & Row.

Anderson, L. W. (1987a). The decline of teacher autonomy: Tears or cheers. *International Review of Education, 33,* 357-373.

Anderson, L. W. (1987b). Developing and using assignments: A key to better instruction. *Effective Schools Report, 5*(4), 1, 4.

Anderson, L. W. (1991). *Increasing teacher effectiveness.* Paris, France: UNESCO International Institute for Educational Planning.

Anderson, L. W. (1993). What time tells us. In L. W. Anderson & H. J. Walberg (Eds.), *Time piece: Extending and enhancing learning time* (pp. 15-22). Reston, VA: National Association of Secondary School Principals.

Anderson, L. W. (1994). Research on teaching and teacher education. In L. W. Anderson & L. A. Sosniak (Eds.), *Bloom's taxonomy: A forty-year retrospective* (pp. 126-145). Chicago: National Society for the Study of Education.

Anderson, L. W., & Jones, B. F. (1981). Designing instructional strategies to facilitate learning for mastery. *Instructional Psychologist, 16,* 121-138.

219

Anderson, L. W., & Pellicer, L. O. (1990). Research synthesis on compensatory and remedial education programs. *Educational Leadership, 48*(1), 10-16.

Anderson, L. W., & Shirley, J. R. (in press). School administrators and educational reform: Lessons learned from a study of South Carolina Re: Learning. *Educational Administration Quarterly.*

Anderson, L. W., & Sosniak, L. A. (Eds.). (1994). *Bloom's taxonomy: A forty-year retrospective.* Chicago: University of Chicago Press.

Ausubel, D. (1968). *Educational psychology: A cognitive view.* New York: Holt, Rinehart & Winston.

Bachman, J. G., Bowers, D. G., & Marcus, P. M. (1968). Bases of supervisory power: A comparative study in five organizational settings. In A. Tannenbaum (Ed.), *Control in organizations* (pp. 229-238). New York: McGraw-Hill.

Bachman, J. G., Smith, C. G., & Slesinger, J. A. (1968). Control, performance, and satisfaction: An analysis of structural and individual effects. In A. Tannenbaum (Ed.), *Control in organizations* (pp. 213-227). New York: McGraw-Hill.

Ballinger, C. (1993). Year round education: It's about time. In L. W. Anderson & H. J. Walberg (Eds.), *Time piece: Extending and enhancing learning time* (pp. 30-34). Reston, VA: National Association of Secondary School Principals.

Barker, R. (1964). *Ecological psychology.* Stanford, CA: Stanford University Press.

Bartlett, J. (1992). *Familiar quotations* (16th ed., J. Kaplan, Ed.). Boston: Little, Brown. (Original work published 1882)

Berliner, D. (1983). The executive functions of teaching. *Instructor, 43*(2), 28-40.

Berliner, D. (1988). Asking questions. In L. W. Anderson (Ed.), *The effective teacher: A video telecourse* [Videotape]. Columbia: South Carolina Educational Television and the University of South Carolina.

Berliner, D. C. (1989). Time to learn. In L. W. Anderson (Ed.), *The effective teacher* (pp. 49-50). New York: McGraw-Hill.

Berliner, D. C. (1994). Teacher expertise. In T. Husen & T. N. Postlethwaite (Eds.), *International encyclopedia of education* (2nd ed., pp. 6020-6026). New York: Pergamon.

Bidwell, C. (1965). The school as a formal organization. In J. March (Ed.), *Handbook of organizations* (pp. 972-1022). Chicago: Rand McNally.

Bloom, B. S. (Ed.). (1956). *Taxonomy of educational objectives: The classification of educational goals. Handbook I: Cognitive domain.* New York: David McKay.

Bloom, B. S. (1965). *Stability and change in human characteristics.* New York: McGraw-Hill.

Bloom, B. S. (1968). Learning for mastery [Entire issue]. *UCLA Evaluation Comment, 2(1).*

Bloom, B. S. (1976). *Human characteristics and school learning.* New York: McGraw-Hill.

Bloom, B. S. (1981). *All our children learning.* New York: McGraw-Hill.

Brandt, R. (1982). On improving teacher effectiveness: A conversation with David Berliner. *Educational Leadership, 40(1),* 12-15.

Bruner, J. S. (1960). *The process of education.* New York: John Wiley.

Bruner, J. S. (1979). *Beyond the information given.* New York: John Wiley.

Burke, P., Christenson, J., & Fessler, R. (1984). *Teacher career stages: Implications for staff development.* Bloomington, IN: Phi Delta Kappa.

Burns, R. B. (1984). How time is used in elementary schools: The activity structure of classrooms. In L. W. Anderson (Ed.), *Time and school learning: Theory, research, and practice* (pp. 91-127). London: Croom Helm.

Carnegie Foundation for the Advancement of Teaching. (1986). *A nation prepared: Teachers for the 21st century* (Report of the Carnegie Task Force on Teaching as a Profession). New York: Carnegie Forum on Education and the Economy.

Clark, C. M., & Peterson, P. L. (1986). Teachers' thought processes. In M. C. Wittrock (Ed.), *Handbook of research on teaching* (3rd ed., pp. 255-296). New York: Macmillan.

Clark, C. M., & Yinger, R. (1989). The hidden world of teaching: Implications of research on teacher planning. In L. W. Anderson (Ed.), *The effective teacher: Study guide and readings* (pp. 223-232). New York: McGraw-Hill.

Cogan, M. L. (1973). *Clinical supervision.* Boston: Houghton Mifflin.

Colburn, A. (1993). *Creating professional development schools.* Bloomington, IN: Phi Delta Kappa.

Connelly, F. M., & Clandinin, D. J. (1993). Cycles, rhythms, and the meaning of school time. In L. W. Anderson & H. J. Walberg (Eds.), *Time piece: Extending and enhancing learning time* (pp. 9-14). Reston, VA: National Association of Secondary School Principals.

Cook, D. L. (1971). *Program evaluation and review technique: Applications in education.* Washington, DC: U.S. Office of Education.

Cooper, J. (1994). Teacher education. In T. Husen & T. N. Postlethwaite (Eds.), *International encyclopedia of education* (2nd ed., pp. 6000-6004). New York: Pergamon.

Cox, H., & Wood, J. R. (1980). Organizational structure and professional alienation: The case of public school teachers. *Peabody Journal of Education, 58*(1), 1-6.

Cuban, L. (1984a). *How teachers taught.* New York: Longman.

Cuban, L. (1984b). School reform by remote control: SB813 in California. *Phi Delta Kappan, 66,* 213-215.

Dahloff, U. S. (1971). *Ability grouping, content validity, and curriculum process analysis.* New York: Teachers College Press.

Dalellew, T., & Martinez, Y. (1988). Andragogy and development: A search for the meaning of staff development. *Journal of Staff Development, 9*(3), 28-31.

Darling-Hammond, L. (1984). *Beyond the commission reports: The coming crisis in teaching.* Santa Monica, CA: Rand Corporation.

Deal, T. E., & Celotti, L. D. (1977). *Loose coupling and school administrators: Some recent research findings.* Stanford, CA: Stanford Center for Research and Development in Teaching. (ERIC Document Reproduction Service No. ED 140 436)

Desrochers, C. G., & Klein, S. R. (1990). Teacher-directed peer coaching as a follow-up to staff development. *Journal of Staff Development, II*(2), 6-10.

Dewey, J. (1929). *Experience and nature.* New York: G. P. Putnam.

Dewey, J. (1933). *How we think.* Lexington, MA: D. C. Heath.

Doyle, W. (1979). Classroom tasks and students' abilities. In P. L. Peterson & H. J. Walberg (Eds.), *Research on teaching: Concepts, findings, and implications* (pp. 183-209). Berkeley, CA: McCutchan.

Dreeben, R. (1968). *On what is learned in schools.* Chicago: University of Chicago Press.

English, F. W. (1993). Changing the cosmology of the school schedule. In L. W. Anderson & H. J. Walberg (Eds.), *Time piece: Extending and enhancing learning time* (pp. 23-29). Reston, VA: National Association of Secondary School Principals.

Farrell, J. P. (1989). International lessons for school effectiveness: The view from the developing world. In M. Holmes, K. A. Leithwood, & D. F. Musella (Eds.), *Educational policy for effective schools* (pp. 53-70). New York: Teachers College Press.

Firestone, W. A., & Pennell, J. R. (1993). Teacher commitment, working conditions, and differential incentive policies. *Review of Educational Research, 63,* 489-525.

Flanders, N. A. (1965). *Teacher influence, pupil attitudes, and achievement.* (U.S. Department of Health, Education and Welfare and the Office of Education Cooperative Research Monograph No. 12). Washington, DC: Government Printing Office.

French, J. R. P., & Raven, B. (1960). The bases of social power. In D. Cartwright & A. F. Zander (Eds.), *Group dynamics: Research and theory* (p. 612). Evanston, IL: Row Peterson.

Fullan, M. G., with Stiegelbauer, S. (1991). *The new meaning of educational change.* New York: Teachers College Press.

Gage, N. L. (1978). *The scientific basis for the art of teaching.* New York: Teachers College Press.

Gagne, R. (1974). *Essentials of learning for instruction.* Hinsdale, IL: Dryden.

Gagne, R., & Briggs, L. (1974). *Principles of instructional design.* New York: Harcourt Brace Jovanovich.

Gall, M. (1970). The use of questions in teaching. *Review of Educational Research, 40,* 707-721.

Galluzo, G. R. (1994). Teacher education, evaluation in. In T. Husen & T. N. Postlethwaite (Eds.), *International encyclopedia of education* (2nd ed., pp. 5954-5958). New York: Pergamon.

Galvez-Hjornevik, G. (1986). Synthesis of research on mentoring beginning teachers. *Journal of Teacher Education, 37*(1), 6-11.

Gardner, J. (1964). *Self-renewal.* New York: Harper & Row.

Gardner, R. (1994). Teacher education, onservice. In T. Husen & T. N. Postlethwaite (Eds.), *International encyclopedia of education* (2nd ed., pp. 5977-5982). New York: Pergamon.

Giammatteo, M. C., & Giammatteo, D. M. (1981). *Forces on leadership*. Reston, VA: National Association of Secondary School Principals.

Gibb, J. R. (1964). Is help helpful? *Forum and Section Journals, 45*(2), 289-293.

Giffen, K., & Patton, B. R. (1974). *Personal communication in human relations*. New York: Merrill/Macmillan.

Gingiss, P. L. (1992). Enhancing program implementation and maintenance through a multiphase approach to peer-based staff development. *Journal of School Health, 62*(5), 161-166.

Ginott, H. (1972). *Teacher and child*. New York: Macmillan.

Ginsberg, R., & Bennett, A. (1981). I don't get no respect. *Vocational Education, 56*, 34-36.

Glatthorn, A. (1984). *Differentiated supervision*. Reston, VA: Association for Supervision and Curriculum Development.

Glatthorn, A. (1994). Teacher development. In T. Husen & T. N. Postlethwaite (Eds.), *International encyclopedia of education* (2nd ed., pp. 5930-5935). New York: Pergamon.

Glickman, C. D. (1981). *Developmental supervision: Alternative practices for helping teachers improve instruction*. Reston, VA: Association for Supervision and Curriculum Development.

Goldhammer, R. (1969). *Clinical supervision*. New York: Holt, Rinehart & Winston.

Good, T. (1981). Teacher expectations and student perceptions: A decade of research. *Educational Leadership, 38*, 415-421.

Goodlad, J. I. (1984). *A place called school*. New York: McGraw-Hill.

Greenfield, W. B. (Ed.). (1987). *Instructional leadership: Concepts, issues, and controversies*. Boston: Allyn & Bacon.

Greenleaf, R. K. (1977). *Servant leadership*. New York: Paulist Press.

Griffin, G. A. (1983). Introduction: The work of staff development. In G. A. Griffin (Ed.), *Staff development. Eighty-second yearbook of the National Society for the Study of Education* (pp. 1-12). Chicago: University of Chicago Press.

Guskey, T. R. (1985a). *Implementing mastery learning*. Belmont, CA: Wadsworth.

Guskey, T. R. (1985b). Staff development and teacher change. *Educational Leadership, 42*(7), 57-60.

Guskey, T. R. (1994). Mastery learning. In T. Husen & T. N. Postlethwaite (Eds.), *International encyclopedia of education* (2nd ed., pp. 3625-3631). New York: Pergamon.

Hatfield, R. C., Blackman, C., Claypool, C., & Master, F. (1987). *Extended professional roles of teacher leaders in the public schools.* Unpublished manuscript, Michigan State University, East Lansing.

Healy, C. C., & Welchert, A. J. (1990). Mentoring relations: A definition to advance research and practice. *Educational Researcher, 19,*(9), 17-21.

Heller, M. (1991). *Developing an effective teacher mentor program* (Phi Delta Kappan Fastbacks, 319, 7-23). Bloomington, IN: Phi Delta Kappa Educational Foundation. (ERIC Document Reproduction Service No. ED 332 996)

Huling-Austin, L. (1992). Research on learning to teach: Implications for teacher induction and mentoring programs. *Journal of Teacher Education, 43*(3), 173-180.

Hunter, M. (1976). *Improved instruction*. El Segundo, CA: TIP.

Husen, T. (Ed.). (1967). *International study of achievement in mathematics* (Vols. 1, 2). New York: John Wiley.

Informal Committee Appointed by the Progressive Education Association to Report on Evaluation of Newer Practices in Education. (1942). *New methods versus old in American education*. New York: Columbia University Teachers College, Bureau of Publications.

Jackson, P. W. (1968). *Life in classrooms*. New York: Teachers College Press.

Jackson, P. W. (1986). *The practice of teaching*. New York: Teachers College Press.

Jackson, P. W. (1988). Asking questions. In L. W. Anderson (Ed.), *The effective teacher: A video telecourse* [Videotape]. Columbia: South Carolina Educational Television and the University of South Carolina.

Jackson, P. W. (1989). *The practice of teaching* (2nd ed.). New York: Teachers College Press.

Johnson, D., & Johnson, R. (1989). Cooperative learning. In L. W. Anderson (Ed.), *The effective teacher* (pp. 175-184). New York: McGraw-Hill.

Joyce, B., & Showers, B. (1982). The coaching of teaching. *Educational Leadership, 40*(1), 4-10.

Knowles, M. S. (1980). *The modern practice of adult education: From pedagogy to andragogy.* Chicago: Association/Follett.

Knowles, M. S. (1984). *Andragogy in action: Applying modern principles of adult learning.* San Francisco: Jossey-Bass.

Knowles, M. S. (1990). *The adult learner: A neglected species.* Houston, TX: Gulf.

Kouzes, J. M., & Posner, B. Z. (1990). *The leadership challenge.* San Francisco: Jossey-Bass.

Krathwohl, D. R. (1985). *Social and behavioral science research.* San Francisco: Jossey-Bass.

Kunisawa, B. N. (1988). A nation in crisis: The dropout dilemma. *NEA Today, 6,* 61-65.

Lambert, M. (1994). Seating arrangements. In T. Husen & T. N. Postlethwaite (Eds.), *International encyclopedia of education* (2nd ed., pp. 5355-5359). New York: Pergamon.

Lieberman, A. (1988). Expanding the leadership team. *Educational Leadership, 45*(5), 4-8.

Lieberman, A., Saxl, E. R., & Miles, M. (1988). Teacher leadership: Ideology and practice. In A. Lieberman (Ed.), *Building a professional culture in schools* (pp. 148-166). New York: Teachers College Press.

Lieberman, M. (1956). *Education as a profession.* Englewood Cliffs, NJ: Prentice Hall.

Little, J. (1988). Assessing the prospects for teacher leadership. In A. Lieberman (Ed.), *Building a professional culture in schools* (pp. 78-106). New York: Teachers College Press.

Livingston, C. (1992). Introduction: Teacher leadership for restructured schools. In C. Livingston (Ed.), *Teachers as leaders: Evolving roles* (pp. 9-17). Washington, DC: National Education Association.

Lortie, D. C. (1975). *Schoolteacher: A sociological study.* Chicago: University of Chicago Press.

Lynch, M., & Strodl, P. (1991, February). *Teacher leadership: Preliminary development of a questionnaire.* Paper presented at the Conference of the Eastern Educational Research Association, Boston.

Marso, R., & Pigge, F. (1990, February). *Teacher mentor induction programs: An assessment by first-year teachers.* Paper presented at the Annual Meeting of the Association of Teacher Educators, Las Vegas, NV. (ERIC Document Reproduction Service No. ED 322-114)

Maslach, C., Jackson, S. E., with Schwab, R. L. (1986). *The Maslach Burnout Inventory manual.* Palo Alto, CA: Consulting Psychologists Press.

Maslow, A. H. (1968). *Toward a psychology of being.* New York: Van Nostrand Reinhold.

McClelland, D. (1975). *Power: The inner experience.* New York: Irvington.

McGreal, T. (1983). Planning. In *Successful teacher evaluation* (pp. 80-84). Alexandria, VA: Association for Supervision and Curriculum Development.

McLaughlin, M., Pfeifer, D., Swanson-Owens, D., & Yee, S. (1986). Why teachers won't teach. *Phi Delta Kappan, 67*(6), 420-427.

Meinick, S. (1989). Self-perceived need for staff development: Are we really getting better as we get older? *Educational Researcher Quarterly, 13*(4), 18-26.

Merriam, S. (1993). Adult learning: Where have we come from? Where are we headed? *New Directions for Adult and Continuing Education, 57,* 5-13.

Meyer, J., & Rowan, B. (1978). The structure of educational organizations. In J. Meyer (Ed.), *Environments and organizations* (pp. 79-109). San Francisco: Jossey-Bass.

Mohlman, G. G., Kierstead, J., & Gundlach, M. (1982). A research-based inservice model for secondary teachers. *Educational Leadership, 40*(1), 16-19.

Moore, J. R. (1988). Guidelines concerning adult learning. *Journal of Staff Development, 9*(3), 2-5.

Morine-Dershimer, G., & Vallance, E. (1976). *Teacher planning* (Beginning Teacher Evaluation Study, Special Report C). San

Francisco: Far West Laboratory for Educational Research and Development.

Muncey, D., & McQuillan, P. (1993). Preliminary findings from a five year study of the Coalition of Essential Schools. *Phi Delta Kappan, 74*(6), 486-489.

National Association of Secondary School Principals (NASSP). (1991). Individual staff development for school renewal. *The Practitioner, XVII*(4), 1-5.

National Commission on Excellence in Education (NCEE). (1983). *A nation at risk: The imperative for educational reform.* Washington, DC: Government Printing Office.

Oakes, J. (1985). *Keeping track: How schools structure inequality.* New Haven, CT: Yale University Press.

O'Connor, K., & Boles, K. (1992, April). *Assessing the needs of teacher leaders in Massachusetts.* Paper presented at the Annual Meeting of the American Educational Research Association, San Francisco.

Odell, S. J. (1990). *Mentor teacher programs: What research says to the teacher.* Washington, DC: National Education Association. (ERIC Document Reproduction Service No. ED 323 185)

Oliva, P. F. (1993). *Supervision for today's schools.* New York: Longman.

Parish, R., & Arends, R. (1983). Why innovative programs are discontinued. *Educational Leadership, 40,* 62-65.

Pellicer, L. O., Anderson, L. W., Keefe, J. W., Kelley, E. A., & McCleary, L. (1990). *High school leaders and their schools: Volume II. Profiles of effectiveness.* Reston, VA: National Association of Secondary School Principals.

Phillips, M. D., & Glickman, C. D. (1991). Peer coaching: Developmental approach to enhancing teaching thinking. *Journal of Staff Development, 12*(2), 20-25.

Polya, G. (1960). *How to solve it.* New York: Harper & Row.

Popham, W. J. (1982). *Modern educational measurement.* Boston: Allyn & Bacon.

Posner, G. (1994). Curriculum planning models. In T. Husen & T. N. Postlethwaite (Eds.), *International encyclopedia of education* (2nd ed., pp. 1328-1334). New York: Pergamon.

Pratt, D. (1980). *Curriculum: Design and development.* New York: Harcourt Brace Jovanovich.

Rauth, M., & Bowers, G. R. (1986). Reaction to induction articles. *Journal of Teacher Education, 37*(1), 38-41.

Reed, S., & Sautter, C. (1990). Children of poverty: The status of 12 million young Americans. *Kappan, 71,* Kl-K12.

Rist, R. C. (1970). Student social class and teacher expectations: The self-fulfilling prophecy in ghetto education. *Harvard Education Review, 40,* 411-451.

Rosenshine, B. V. (1986). Synthesis of research on explicit teaching. *Educational Leadership, 43,* 60-69.

Rothkopf, E. Z. (1976). Writing to teach and reading to learn: A perspective on the psychologies of written instruction. In N. L. Gage & D. C. Berliner (Eds.), *The psychology of teaching method* (pp. 91-129). Chicago: University of Chicago Press.

Rowan, B., & Guthrie, L. F. (1989). The quality of Chapter I instruction: Results from a study of twenty-four schools. In R. E. Slavin, N. L. Karweit, & N. A. Madden (Eds.), *Effective programs for students at risk* (pp. 195-219). Boston: Allyn & Bacon.

Rowe, M. B. (1972, April). *Wait time and rewards as instructional variables: Their influence on language, logic, and fate control.* Paper presented at the National Association for Research in Science Teaching, Chicago.

Ryan, D. W. (1983). Redefining the roles of middle managers in outcome-based systems. *Outcomes, 2*(4), 26-33.

Sadker, M., & Sadker, D. (1986). Sexism in the classroom: From grade school to graduate school. *Kappan, 67,* 512-515.

Sanders, N. M. (1966). *Classroom questions: Why kinds?* New York: Harper & Row.

Schwille, J., Porter, A., Belli, G., Floden, R., Freeman, D., Knappen, L., Kuhs, T., & Schmidt, W. (1983). Teachers as policy brokers in the content of elementary school mathematics. In L. S. Shulman & G. Sykes (Eds.), *Handbook of teaching and policy* (pp. 370-391). New York: Longman.

Scriven, M. (1967). The methodology of evaluation. In R. Tyler, R. Gagne, & M. Scriven (Eds.), *Perspectives on curriculum evaluation* (pp. 39-83). Chicago: Rand McNally.

Sergiovanni, T., & Starratt, R. (1971). *Emerging patterns of supervision: Human perspectives.* New York: McGraw-Hill.

Shedd, J., & Bacharach, S. (1991). *Tangled hierarchies: Teachers as professionals and the management of schools.* San Francisco: Jossey-Bass.

Shostak, R. (1986). Lesson presentation skills. In J. M. Cooper (Ed.), *Classroom teaching skills* (pp. 111-137). Lexington, MA: D.C. Heath.

Shulman, L. S. (1983). Autonomy and obligation: The remote control of teaching. In L. S. Shulman & G. Sykes (Eds.), *Handbook of teaching and policy* (pp. 484-504). New York: Longman.

Silberman, C. (1970). *Crisis in the classroom.* New York: Basic Books.

Sirotnik, K. A. (1985, April). *Responsibility vs. accountability: Toward a professional teaching profession.* Paper presented to the American Educational Research Association, Chicago.

Sirotnik, K. A. (1987). Evaluation in the ecology of schooling: The process of school renewal. In J. I. Goodlad (Ed.), *The ecology of school renewal* (pp. 41-62). Chicago: University of Chicago Press.

Sizer, T. (1984). *Horace's compromise.* Boston: Houghton Mifflin.

Sizer, T. (1988). A visit to an "Essential School." *School Administrator, 45*(10), 18-19.

Slavin, R. E. (1994). Cooperative learning. In T. Husen & T. N. Postlethwaite (Eds.), *International encyclopedia of education* (2nd ed., pp. 235-238). New York: Pergamon.

Smith, B. O. (1987). Definitions of teaching. In M. J. Dunkin (Ed.), *International encyclopedia of teaching and teacher education* (pp. 11-15). New York: Pergamon.

Sparks, D. (1990). Cognitive coaching: An interview with Robert Garmston. *Journal of Staff Development, II*(2), 12-15.

Stodolsky, S. S. (1988). *The subject matters.* Chicago: University of Chicago Press.

Sykes, G. (1983). Public policy and the problem of teacher quality: The need for screens and magnets. In L. S. Shulman & G. Sykes (Eds.), *Handbook of teaching and policy* (pp. 97-125). New York: Longman.

Sykes, G. (1987, April). *Teaching incentives: Constraint and variety.* Paper presented at the American Educational Research Association Conference, Washington, DC.

Tannenbaum, A. (1968). *Control in organizations.* New York: McGraw-Hill.

Tanner, D., & Tanner, L. N. (1975). *Curriculum development: Theory into practice.* New York: Macmillan.

Thomas, D. (1975). Education's seven deadly myths. *NASSP Bulletin, 59,* 61.

Tobin, W. (1987). The role of wait time in higher cognitive learning. *Review of Educational Research, 57,* 69-95.

Torper, U. (1994). Frame factors. In T. Husen & T. N. Postlethwaite (Eds.), *International encyclopedia of education* (2nd ed., pp. 2375-2377). New York: Pergamon.

Troen, V., & Boles, K. (1994). A time to lead. *Teacher Magazine,* pp. 40-41.

Tyler, R. W. (1949). *Basic principles of curriculum and instruction.* Chicago: University of Chicago Press.

Veenman, S. (1984). Perceived problems of beginning teachers. *Review of Educational Research, 54*(2), 143-178.

Wagner, A. (1994). Teacher education, economics of. In T. Husen & T. N. Postlethwaite (Eds.), *International encyclopedia of education* (2nd ed., pp. 5948-5954). New York: Pergamon.

Wasley, P. (1991). *Teachers who lead: The rhetoric of reform and the realities of practice.* New York: Teachers College Press.

Weick, K. E. (1976). Educational organizations as loosely coupled systems. *Administrative Science Quarterly, 21*(1), 1-29.

Westbury, I. (1989). The problems of comparing curriculums across educational systems. In A. C. Purves (Ed.), *International comparisons and educational reform* (pp. 17-34). Washington, DC: ASCD.

Yinger, R. J. (1994). Teacher planning, approaches to. In T. Husen & T. N. Postlethwaite (Eds.), *International encyclopedia of education* (2nd ed., pp. 6031-6035). New York: Pergamon.

Zumwalt, K. (1989). Beginning professional teachers: The need for a curricular vision of teaching. In M. Reynolds (Ed.), *Knowledge base for the beginning teacher* (pp. 173-184). New York: Pergamon.

Index

Printed in the United States
920100003B

9 780803 961739